D1489664

At Issue

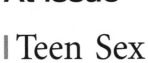

| Teen Sex

Other Books in the At Issue Series:

At Issue

▍Teen Sex

Olivia Ferguson, Book Editor

GREENHAVEN PRESS
A part of Gale, Cengage Learning

GALE
CENGAGE Learning™

Detroit • New York • San Francisco • New Haven, Conn • Waterville, Maine • London

GALE
CENGAGE Learning™

Christine Nasso, *Publisher*
Elizabeth Des Chenes, *Managing Editor*

© 2011 Greenhaven Press, a part of Gale, Cengage Learning.

Gale and Greenhaven Press are registered trademarks used herein under license.

For more information, contact:
Greenhaven Press
27500 Drake Rd.
Farmington Hills, MI 48331-3535
Or you can visit our Internet site at gale.cengage.com

For product information and technology assistance, contact us at

Gale Customer Support, 1-800-877-4253
For permission to use material from this text or product, submit all requests online at www.cengage.com/permissions

Further permissions questions can be e-mailed to permissionrequest@cengage.com

Articles in Greenhaven Press anthologies are often edited for length to meet page requirements. In addition, original titles of these works are changed to clearly present the main thesis and to explicitly indicate the author's opinion. Every effort is made to ensure that Greenhaven Press accurately reflects the original intent of the authors. Every effort has been made to trace the owners of copyrighted material.

Cover image © Images.com/Corbis.

LIBRARY OF CONGRESS CATALOGING-IN-PUBLICATION DATA

Teen sex / Olivia Ferguson, book editor.
   p. cm. -- (At issue)
Includes bibliographical references and index.
ISBN 978-0-7377-5095-9 (hbk.) -- ISBN 978-0-7377-5096-6 (pbk.)
1. Teenagers--Sexual behavior--Juvenile literature. 2. Sexual abstinence--Juvenile literature. 3. Sexual ethics for teenagers--Juvenile literature. I. Ferguson, Olivia.
HQ27.T3873 2010
306.70835--dc22
                                                          2010022997

Printed in the United States of America
1 2 3 4 5 6 7 14 13 12 11 10

Contents

Introduction

One of the issues regarding teen sex that must be considered but is often overlooked during both abstinence-only education and comprehensive sex education is that of the age of consent, the age at which it is actually legal for young people to consent to sexual intercourse. Many of the preteens and teens who are being taught about abstinence, contraceptives, and sexually transmitted diseases would actually be committing a crime if they were to become sexually active, depending on their age and that of their partner. This important information would benefit the curriculum because the punishment for this crime can have a long-lasting effect on someone's life, and though there are people who are fighting to have age of consent laws reevaluated and updated, there are others who feel such laws are not harsh enough.

Age of consent laws vary from state to state. In some states teens can have sex as early as fourteen, but only with someone within two years of their age. In other states—New York, for example—two sixteen-year-olds engaging in sexual activity are considered to be committing a sexual crime against each other. In his article "Embracing Teenage Sexuality: Let's Rethink the Age of Consent," Jacob M. Appel writes that "These draconian and puritanical laws are largely the product of a conservative political culture that has transformed the fight against child molestation into a full-blown war on teenage sexuality." He continues his article by discussing how other countries are raising the effective age in age of consent laws to bring them up to date with today's culture, but the United States keeps its age of consent laws as they are, causing sexually active teenagers to be put into the same category as "clergymen who rape toddlers."

Appel isn't the only one who thinks that something needs to be done about age of consent laws in the United States.

Psychologist, professor, and author Robert Epstein reiterated the criticism of these laws, telling *Lodi News-Sentinel* staff writer Layla Bohm that he "really assumed the laws would be similar, and they are not. There's an insanity to them." For example, in California a nineteen-year-old sleeping with a seventeen-year-old can be prosecuted for statutory rape and be labeled as a sex offender for the rest of his or her life, but it is perfectly legal to be forty and date an eighteen-year-old.

On the other side of the debate are those who disagree with lowering the age of consent and instead feel it should be raised to eighteen. They feel that doing so would offer more protection from child predators as well as ensure that an individual is emotionally ready to make the decision of whether to have sex. In an interview with the *Daily Mail* newspaper, Mandy Smith, former underage lover and ex-wife of Rolling Stones bassist Bill Wyman, confessed her regrets over becoming sexually active as early as she did. She argues that "It's not about being physically mature. It's emotional maturity that matters" and expresses her concern for the young girls who are forced to grow up in today's sexualized society. She also thinks that some girls, even at eighteen, are not emotionally mature enough to consent to sex.

Although the tendency in the United Kingdom has been to lower the age of consent, there are some individuals who are expressing concern. Northern Ireland's Legislative Assembly was upset about the decision to lower the age of consent to sixteen, citing the likelihood of child predators to move north in search of victims. The Belfast Rape Crisis Center also feels that this lowering of the age of consent will make it harder to protect young teens. The reasoning behind Parliament's move to lower the age of consent was to make Northern Ireland's age of consent coincide with the rest of the kingdom, which in turn eliminates some of the confusion.

While the debate continues about what the correct age of consent should be, many people agree this is a topic that should be added to the sex education curriculum, be it abstinence or comprehensive. Young people can be made aware that there are in fact laws as well as consequences that go along with breaking them.

1

Teen Sex: An Overview

Henry J. Kaiser Family Foundation

The Henry J. Kaiser Family Foundation is a private, nonprofit foundation that focuses on the major health care issues in the United States as well as the U.S. role internationally in health care.

After being in decline during the last decade, the number of sexually active teens has hit a plateau. Research also shows a high percentage of young adults and teens with STIs (sexually transmitted infections) and teen pregnancies again on the rise, after having been in a slow decline during the past decade. Some of the research shows that males are only slightly more likely than females to report having sex, and that many teens do not realize that oral sex can be just as dangerous in spreading STIs. Studies have also shown that despite declines in the past decade, the United States still has high teen pregnancy, birth, and abortion rates when compared to the rest of the developed world.

Following a decade of decline, the [number] of adolescents engaging in sexual activity has leveled off in recent years. Recent data indicate that sexually transmitted infection rates are very high for young adults and that teen birth rates may be trending upwards after years of steady decline. This fact sheet provides key data on teen and young adult sexual activity rates, pregnancy and birth rates, contraceptive use, and

The Henry J. Kaiser Family Foundation, "Sexual Health of Adolescents and Young Adults in the United States," *Kaiser Family Foundation*, September 2008. This information was reprinted with permission of the Henry J. Kaiser Family Foundation. The Kaiser Family Foundation is a non-profit private operating foundation, based in Menlo Park, California, dedicated to producing and communicating the best possible analysis and information on health issues.

prevalence of sexually transmitted infections. It also discusses some of the central policies that affect access to reproductive health care services for youth.

Many young adults consider oral sex to be less risky in terms of health, social, and emotional consequences than vaginal sex.

Sexual Activity

Nearly half (48%) of all high school students in 2007 reported ... having had sexual intercourse, a decline from 54% in 1991. Males (50%) are slightly more likely than females (46%) to report having had sex. The median age at first intercourse is 16.9 years for boys and 17.4 years for girls.

There are racial/ethnic differences in sexual activity rates. African-American high school students are more likely to have had intercourse (67%) compared to White (44%) and Hispanic students (52%). 16% of African-American high school students and 8% of Latino students initiated sex before age 13 compared to 4% of White students.

Many young adults consider oral sex to be less risky in terms of health, social, and emotional consequences than vaginal [intercourse]. Over half of males (55%) and females (54%) ages 15 to 19 report having had oral sex with someone of the opposite sex. About 24% of males and 22% of females ages 15–19 had oral sex but not vaginal intercourse.

Approximately one in 10 males and females ages 15 to 19 have engaged in anal sex with someone of the opposite sex; and about 5% of males ages 15 to 19 have had oral or anal sex with a male.

The percentage of high school students who report having had four or more sexual partners declined from 18% in 1995 to 15% in 2007. Males (18%) are more likely than females (12%) to report having had four or more sexual partners.

Among those ages 20 to 24, males have a higher average number of partners (3.8) than females (2.8). Men in this age group are also more likely (30%) than women (21%) to report having had seven or more sexual partners.

Almost one-quarter (23%) of currently sexually active high school students reported using alcohol or drugs during their most recent sexual encounter, with males having a higher percentage (28%) compared to females (18%).

One in 10 high school students reported having experienced dating violence. Nine percent of students have been physically forced to have sexual intercourse, with females (11%) more likely than males (5%) to report this experience.

The average age of first marriage continues to rise, reaching 25.6 for women and 27.5 for men in 2007.

Pregnancy

Despite the decline in teen pregnancy rates over the past decade, the U.S. continues to have [some] of the highest teen pregnancy, birth, and abortion rates in the developed world.

The teen pregnancy rate fell from 77 pregnancies per 1,000 girls ages 15 to 17 in 1990 to 42 in 2004. The rate also dropped for girls ages 18 to 19 from 168 pregnancies per 1,000 girls in 1990 to 119 in 2004.

However, the teen birth rate increased 3% between 2005 and 2006 to 42 births per 1,000 girls (15–19 years old), the first increase following a long-term decline.

The teen abortion rate has been falling.

By age 20, 32% of Latinas, 24% of African-American women and 21% of Native Americans have [given] birth, compared to 11% of White and 7% of Asian-American women.

Of the approximately 729,000 pregnancies of girls 15 to 19 years old in 2004, 57% ended in live births, 27% in induced abortions and 16% in fetal losses.

The teen abortion rate has been falling. The abortion rate for teens ages 15 to 19 and young adults ages 20 to 24 years old was 19.8 and 39.9 per 1,000 women, respectively, in 2004. About 17% of women having abortions in the U.S. are teens, and 33% are between the ages of 20 and 24.

Thirty-five states require parental involvement in a minor's decision to have an abortion, up from eighteen states in 1991. Twenty-two of these states require parental consent, eleven require parental notification, and two require both.

In contrast, 35 states and [the District of Columbia] allow a minor to obtain confidential prenatal care that includes regular medical visits and routine services for labor and delivery without parental consent or notification. In 12 of these states, however, physicians can inform parents that their minor daughters are seeking or receiving prenatal care, if [such a course of action is] deemed in the best interest of the minor.

Contraceptive Use and Services

In 2007, among the 35% of currently sexually active high school students, 62% reported using a condom the last time they had sexual intercourse, up from 57% in 1997. African-American students (67%) were more likely to report using condoms compared to White (60%) and Hispanic (61%) students. Males (69%) were more like to report condom use than females (55%).

Oral contraceptive use was much lower, with 16% of currently sexually active high school students reporting they or their partner had used birth control pills. White students (21%) were more likely to use birth control pills compared to African-American (9%) and Hispanic (9%) students.

Using a dual method of a condom and hormonal contraceptive is becoming more prevalent for teenage females. The percentage of currently sexually active never-married females 15–19 years of age reporting use of dual methods rose from 8% in 1995 to 20% in 2002.

About one-quarter of teen females and 18% of teen males used no method of contraception at first intercourse. Research has shown that those who reported condom use at their sexual debut were more likely than those who did not use condoms to engage in subsequent protective behaviors.

Emergency contraception can prevent pregnancy when taken shortly after unprotected intercourse. This drug, sold as Plan B, remains a prescription-only drug for minors, but is available as an over-the-counter medication for those aged 18 and older.

Health insurance coverage and the ability to pay directly for services influence teen access to contraceptive services. Older adolescents and young adults have the highest uninsured rate of any age group. Approximately 29% of young adults 18–24 years old were uninsured and 13% were covered by Medicaid in 2006. One-third (32%) of young adults lived below the poverty level and an additional 23% were near-poor (100–199% [of the] federal poverty level).

The federal Title X program funds confidential contraceptive services and STD screening and treatment for low-income teens and young adults by providing funding to approximately 4,600 clinics, public health departments, and hospitals.

Currently, Medicaid provides over six in 10 public dollars for family planning services in the U.S. Twenty-six states operate special Medicaid family planning waiver programs that offer contraceptive services to individuals (mostly women) who otherwise would not qualify for Medicaid. Of those, 20 states provide these benefits to individuals based on income, with most states setting the income eligibility ceiling at or near 200% of [the] poverty [level]. Seventeen states extend their services to all teens.

Confidentiality is important for youth access to health care services. Twenty-one states and DC have enacted policies that explicitly allow all minors to consent to contraceptive services.

Currently, there are 1,700 school-based health centers in the country that provide on-site services including pregnancy testing, STD diagnosis and treatment, and HIV testing and counseling. Contraception is often provided only by referral.

Sexually active adolescents and young adults are at higher risk for acquiring STIs.

Sexually Transmitted Infections (STIs)

Compared to older adults, sexually active adolescents and young adults are at higher risk for acquiring STIs, which is attributable to a combination of behavioral, biological, and cultural factors.

An estimated 9.1 million adolescents and young adults ages 15–24 were newly infected with a STI in 2000 (the most recent year for which data is available), which represented almost one-half of all new STI cases. The Human Papilloma Virus (HPV) was the most common STI (51% of new infections), followed by trichomoniasis (21%) and chlamydia (16%).

An unpublished 2008 CDC [Centers for Disease Control and Prevention] study finds that among female adolescents ages 14 to 19, one in four (26%) . . . has HPV, chlamydia, HSV-2 infection, or trichomoniasis, with HPV accounting for the vast majority of infections. African-American girls had a higher STI prevalence (48%) than Whites (20%) and Latinas (20%).

Despite the higher risk for acquiring STIs among youth, only one-third (31%) of sexually active teens ages 15 to 17, and half (53%) of sexually active young adults ages 18 to 24 say they have been tested for STDs.

In 2006, the Food and Drug Administration approved a new vaccine that protects against infection for certain strains of HPV associated with cervical cancer and genital warts. A CDC advisory committee has recommended that all girls be vaccinated at age 11 or 12, and that girls and women ages 13 to 26 be given a "catch-up" vaccination. A recent CDC survey found that only 10% of women ages 18 to 26 had received the HPV vaccine as of summer 2007.

HIV/AIDS

The CDC estimates that almost 46,000 young people, ages 13 to 24, were living with HIV in the U.S (in the 45 states and 5 dependent areas with confidential name-based HIV reporting) in 2006. Women [constituted] 28% of these HIV/AIDS cases among 13- to 24-year-olds.

African-American young adults are disproportionately affected by HIV infection, accounting for 60% of HIV/AIDS diagnoses in 13- to 24-year-olds in 2006.

More HIV infections occurred among adolescents and young adults 13–29 years old (34% of new HIV infections) than any other age group. Most young people with HIV/AIDS were infected by sexual transmission.

In 2006, 16% of young adults ages 18 to 24 reported that they had been tested for HIV in the past 12 months.

2

Abstinence-Only Sex Education Programs Fail Teens

Eric Alterman and George Zornick

Eric Alterman is a senior fellow at Center for American Progress and the author of Why We're Liberals: A Political Handbook for Post-Bush America, *from which some information in this article has been taken. George Zornick is a writer based in New York.*

In Katy Vine's investigation into the success of sex-education programs in Texas, she found that while Texas receives $4.5 million a year in federal funding for abstinence programs, more than any other state, it is still number one in teenage births. Abstinence-only programs show little to no effect on teens' attitudes toward sex and have a negative effect on their rate of contraceptive use. The failure of these programs is directly related to the fact that they intentionally provide teens with misinformation. Because conservatives refuse to acknowledge this fact, teen pregnancy and birth rates will continue to increase.

The current *Texas Monthly* features an extensive investigation by Katy Vine into the success of the state's sex-education program. Some of its key findings include the startling revelations that:

Eric Alterman and George Zornick, "Think Again: The Costs of Enforced Sexual Ignorance," Center for American Progress, May 8, 2008. This material was created by the Center for American Progress www.americanprogress.org.

- Texas gets more than $4.5 million a year through Title V, a stream of federal funding for abstinence programs—more than any other state.

- The Texas Education Code, written by the state legislature, requires that classrooms give more attention to abstinence than any other approach and that they must present abstinence as the only method that is 100 percent effective at preventing pregnancy, sexually transmitted infections, HIV/AIDS, and the "emotional trauma associated with adolescent sexual activity."

- No law mandates that methods of contraception be included in sex ed classes, and condom instruction is not encouraged anywhere in the code.

- Only one of the four state-approved high school student health textbooks uses the word "condom," and that book reaches only a small percentage of the Texas market.

- "In the entire state we found two people that were involved in these programs that had degrees in health education," Texas A&M researcher, B.E. "Buzz" Pruitt said. "Two of the curricula didn't contain a single fact."

This lack of sex education is certainly taking a toll:

- Texas ranks number one in teenage births, costing taxpayers there over $1 billion a year. And 24 percent of those births are not the girl's first delivery.

- The rate of teenage births in Texas is decreasing at a slower rate than the nation at large.

- Texan teenagers say they are having sex at a higher rate than the national average (52.5 percent vs. 47 percent).

The Texas story is merely an extreme version of a phenomenon that is taking place all around America. Under current federal standards, any sex education program receiving federal funds must conform to "abstinence-only" guidelines, which means mentioning contraception only to discuss its failures, and teaching, among other things, that "sexual activity outside of the context of marriage is likely to have harmful psychological and physical effects."

These programs are chosen as if specifically designed not to work. One long-term evaluation of 10 state abstinence-only programs concluded, "Abstinence-only programs show little evidence of sustained (long-term) impact on attitudes and intentions. Worse, they show some negative impacts on youth's willingness to use contraception, including condoms, to prevent negative sexual health outcomes related to sexual intercourse. Importantly, only in one state did any program demonstrate short-term success in delaying the initiation of sex; none of these programs demonstrates evidence of long-term success in delaying sexual initiation among youth exposed to the programs or any evidence of success in reducing other sexual risk-taking behaviors among participants."

Of course, these programs are less oriented toward giving teenagers reliable information about sexuality than toward indoctrinating them with conservative Christian views about sex. A single grant-making program at the Health Resources and Services Administration, federal aid to abstinence education, for instance, has doled out more than $50 million in federal grants to such organizations as Care Net Pregnancy Services of DuPage, Illinois, an evangelistic organization that exists to help women who experience unplanned or unwanted pregnancies "choose life for their unborn babies"; Door of Hope Pregnancy Care Center in Madisonville, Kentucky, an organization "committed to the belief in the sanctity of human life, primarily as it relates to the protection of the unborn"; and Bethany Crisis Pregnancy Services in Colorado Springs, Colorado, which warns women considering abortion, "Your pregnancy ends with death. You may feel guilt and shame about your choice. You will remember taking a life."

In a larger study by the Centers for Disease Control, researchers found that although teenagers who take "virginity pledges" may wait longer to initiate sexual activity, they are more likely to enjoy oral and anal sex, and they are just as likely as other students to be infected with sexually transmitted diseases. Eighty-eight percent eventually have premarital intercourse. While abstinence-only programs show little evidence of sustained effect on a student's sexual activities, they do reduce the use of contraception, including condoms, when sex does take place.

The large-scale failure of these programs is at least partially attributable to the fact that they are purposely, indeed transparently, dishonest. Of the 13 federally funded programs studied in a minority staff report by the Committee on Government Reform, just two provided students with accurate medical and scientific information, a finding that was consistent with a U.S. Government Accountability Office study released two years later. In the rest, students learned such "facts" as:

- Half the gay male teenagers in the United States have tested positive for the AIDS virus.

- Touching a person's genitals "can result in pregnancy."

- A 43-day-old fetus is a "thinking person."

- HIV, the virus that causes AIDS, can be spread via sweat and tears.

- Condoms fail to prevent HIV transmission as often as 31 percent of the time in heterosexual intercourse. (The actual rate is less than 3 percent, according to the Centers for Disease Control.)

- Women who experience abortions "are more prone to suicide," and as many as 10 percent of them become sterile.

The right-wingers who continue to promote these programs refuse to accept that their false information is in any way responsible for increased pregnancy and STIs. According to the conservative Christians in the Family Research Council, however, the relative failure of their lessons merely indicates that even more of the same may be needed. Upon the announcement that yet another study—this one congressionally mandated and published by Mathematica Policy Research Inc. in the spring of 2007—had demonstrated the ineffectiveness of such education, the group insisted that these very same failed "programs must be intensive and long-term, so that the knowledge, attitudes, and skills needed to reject sex before marriage are constantly reinforced—particularly in the pivotal high school years."

Abstinence-only programs show little evidence of sustained (long-term) impact on attitudes and intentions.

By way of comparison, Canadian and European young people are about as active sexually as Americans, but teenage American girls are five times as likely to have a baby as French girls, seven times as likely to have an abortion, and 70 times as likely to have gonorrhea as teenage girls in the Netherlands. In addition, the incidence of HIV/AIDS among American teenagers is five times that of the same age group in Germany. Is it any wonder, therefore, that 17 states have so far chosen to forgo federal matching funds rather than submit their children to the dishonest, propagandistic programs of conservative abstinence-only ideologues toward nearly all forms of sexual activity.

As if to demonstrate where its own priorities in this area lay, in November 2006, the Bush administration nominated Dr. Eric Keroack to the post of deputy assistant secretary for population affairs, overseeing a number of Health and Human Services programs, including the Office of Family Planning and what is called "Title X," a Nixon-era program that distributes contraceptives to poor or uninsured women. A favorite guest speaker of the National Right to Life Committee, Keroack teaches that there is a physiological cause for relationship failure and sexual promiscuity that he calls "God's Super Glue," which results in a hormonal cause and effect that can be short-circuited only by sexual abstinence until marriage.

A tiny, extremist minority in Congress is ensuring that the rate of teenage pregnancy and sexually transmitted diseases remains unnaturally high.

And though he enjoyed the position of full-time medical director for A Woman's Concern, a chain of Boston-area crisis pregnancy centers that regards the distribution of contraceptives as demeaning to women, he was not even a certified obstetrician-gynecologist at the time of his appointment. (Keroack resigned this post shortly after the Massachusetts Office of Medicaid announced an investigation into his private practice.)

What is perhaps most infuriating about the use and abuse of teenagers as proxies for the right's culture war against all forms of non-marital sexuality is the fact that it has little democratic support. An extensive survey by the Kaiser Family Foundation and Harvard University asked voters whether "the federal government should fund sex education programs that have 'abstaining from sexual activity' as their only purpose" or if "the money should be used to fund more comprehensive sex education programs that include information on how to obtain and use condoms and other contraceptives." The condom/contraceptive option won the day by a margin of 67 percent to 30 percent. Unsurprisingly, a similar number (65 percent) said they worried that refusing to provide teens with good information about contraception might lead to unsafe sex, while only 28 percent were more concerned that such information might encourage teens to have sex.

In other words, a tiny, extremist minority in Congress is ensuring that the rate of teenage pregnancy and sexually transmitted diseases remains unnaturally high because it prefers to cling to its ideological dicta rather than accept the facts that demonstrate the cost of its misinformation.

Sound familiar?

Kudos to Ms. Vine and the *Texas Monthly* for helping to illuminate the human side of democratic, scientific, and educational failure.

3

Sex Education Steals Childhood from Pre-Teens

Cassy Fiano

Cassy Fiano is a blogger for Hot Air's the Green room and Stop the ACLU (American Civil Liberties Union). Her posts have also been used on other Web sites such as Right Wing News and Conservative Grapevine, as well as Wizbang.com.

Parents of students at Fort Merriman Middle School in Utah are attempting to have a teacher fired and barred from ever teaching again because of the curriculum of her sex education class. The parents feel that the teacher went too far with her explanations of different types of sexual activity and some her visual aids. Sex education used to be only about the basics, such as body parts and the menstrual cycle. Then, in high school, it became more of a scare tactic to encourage teenagers not to engage in sexual activity. Parents now seem to be trying to encourage their children to grow up too fast, not allowing children to be children for as long as they should.

Wow, things have sure changed since I went to school.

Middle-schoolers at Fort Herriman Middle School in Utah had a, well, *interesting* lesson plan waiting for them which made their parents furious. They were taught all about sex! Europe, here we come . . .

A middle school health teacher is under investigation, accused of teaching too much about sex.

Cassy Fiano, "Sex and the Cafeteria: Teaching Middle-Schoolers How to Have Good Sex," cassyfiano.com, May 29, 2008. Reproduced by permission.

Parents say the teacher is saying crude and explicit things that don't belong in the classroom. Dewayne Smith [said], "These are our children, and we're not going to breach the firewall of innocence."

Parents say sex education went too far inside the classroom full of 8th-graders at Fort Herriman Middle School. Suzanne Johnson told us, "She explained how the teacher talked about masturbation. Girl masturbation, boys, the wrong ways . . . the right ways to have sex, the wrong ways to have sex. How long to make it last. I mean, disgusting."

"What bothered me is that, not only did we get into discussions of masturbatory activity, but we got into explicit descriptions of homosexual acts," Smith said.

Parents say the teacher also showed students fliers with explicit cartoon images.

Seventh-grader Marissa Poloei had a friend in the class. She told us, "He thought it was gross and stuff, and she showed a lot of pictures of stuff."

A spokesperson for the Jordan School District would not comment on the allegations but said there is an investigation. The teacher has been put on administrative leave, but parents don't think that's enough.

Johnson [said], "We want her fired. We want her never to teach ever again."

Some of the parents plan to meet with administrators at the school tomorrow. They've invited [Representative] Carl Wimmer to attend.

Again, the district said it cannot comment on personnel issues. We were not able to contact the teacher for her side of the story.

Kinda reminds me of this ad I . . . remember seeing for *Sex and the City*, except it was the four women when they were middle-schoolers. I couldn't find it on YouTube, but it was basically Carrie, Miranda, Charlotte and Samantha as adolescent girls, already gossiping together and already in their cliched roles.

Is that what this teacher was trying to do? Is that what this class was supposed to be? I can just see this being the newest show on MTV: Sex and the Cafeteria. How to have good sex when you've just hit puberty and can barely get it up or really understand what it is you're doing.

What Sex Education Used to Be

The parents have every right to be outraged, and that teacher—if everything the parents are saying is accurate, and I don't doubt that it is—should be fired. And let me just say this: unlike a lot of conservatives, I actually don't have a problem with *some* sexual education. In my high school, we were required to take it (I had it around my junior year). But it was absolutely nothing like what this teacher is teaching. If anything, sex ed was really a huge scare tactic. We were taught in *terrifying* detail about what different kinds of STDs [sexually transmitted diseases] there are, and what exactly they would do to you.

Children are no longer allowed to be children.

We were taught about what different kinds of birth control were out there, how they worked, what the potential risks to your body were, and how effective they were. Always the teacher stressed that the best way to keep yourself free from STDs and to not get pregnant was to remain abstinent, because even using a condom and birth control was not always foolproof. Best of all, we were told about the emotional and psychological effect having sex when you aren't ready (read: TOO YOUNG) could be, and how devastating it can be. Like I said, that class scared the bejesus out of me. I lived in fear that if I had sex, I would get pregnant, contract syphillis, and be depressed all at the same time. That class never once said that abstinence was the best answer—it stressed personal choice—but it covered every possible base that there was when it came to possible *consequences*. The attitude was that if you're going to do it, you need to be prepared for the risk you're taking.

And you know, I don't really have a problem with a program like that—for *high-schoolers*. I thought it was age-appropriate and made perfect sense. In fifth grade, my sex-ed class consisted of splitting the boys and girls into two different classes. I have no idea what the boys were taught, but we were basically told what would be happening soon, and mainly centered [on] what our monthly visits from Aunt Flo would be like. Again, no arguments from me here.

Adults Are Rushing Children Out of Childhood

But this? Explaining to children how to have sex well, how to make it last longer, how to masturbate, what different kinds of homosexual acts you can practice . . . that's just outrageous. The fact that children are being taught these kinds of things says a lot about where we are as a society today. Children are no longer allowed to be children. They're being asked to grow up and handle adult decisions at earlier and earlier ages, while their parents and teachers either look the other way or encourage them. These are *children*. Let them enjoy their childhood and innocence and naivete and idealism while they can. They don't need to be informed about the many different kinds of sexuality that exist and then encouraged to go out and practice. That'll lead them down a dark, lonely road which will inevitably lead to a lot of anger, cynicism and bitterness.

I seriously wonder why it is that so many adults seem to want to rush children into adulthood. I really just don't understand it. Yesterday I asked if they were just living vicariously. I really do think that excuse is grasping at some pretty frail straws, but this entire debacle about teaching kids to have sex boggles my mind, just like dressing your sixteen-or-under little girl like a porn star boggles my mind.

Really, with this case, one of the parents summed it up best:

> These are our children, and we're not going to breach the firewall of innocence.

Glad to see that there are still *some* parents out there that understand that.

4

Sex Education Is the Key to Curbing Teen Sex

Kate Sawyer

Kate Sawyer is a teacher at Furtherwick Park School on Canvey Island, Essex, England.

England's Personal, Social, and Health Education program, or PSHE, is the mechanism through which teachers deliver sex education to teenagers. The main issue is how to get the right message about sex across to teens and not add to the confusion that already naturally comes with being a teen. Many parents are actually adding to this confusion by mistakenly assuming that their children are already sexually active and putting them on birth control. What all adults, teachers and parents alike, should be doing is setting an example and talking openly and honestly with their children.

When I was first given the job of head of PSHE [Personal, Social, and Health Education] in my comprehensive school, a friend asked me to explain what exactly that entailed. He listened carefully and summed up simply. "I see," he said. "It's all the bits the parents should do."

To a degree he was right. When my brother announced that a male and female rabbit only had to look at each other in different hutches to become pregnant it was our mother, not the school, who overcame blushes and put him right. I doubt there is a single 10-year-old in the land now who thinks rabbits need only look at each other to breed. Not now that half of them are breeding like rabbits themselves.

PSHE—personal, social and health education—recently became PSHEE when the government added "economic well-being and financial capability" to the guidance it feels parents cannot or do not deliver to their children.

I am surrounded by teenagers with their noise, vitality and truculence and, above all, their opinions.

England's Famous Teen Father

You can see why if you listen to Alfie Patten, the nation's latest cheeky chappie. Asked how he will cope financially, having fathered a baby at 13, he replied: "What's financially?"

So what is it all about, Alfie? Are you the victim of lust, a bad family, bad teaching or just bad luck?

It seems as though every expert in England has a point of view about Alfie and where he went wrong. I am not an expert. I am simply a teacher. From offices and libraries the pundits' opinions have poured forth. I am writing from the muck and litter of the average classroom. I am surrounded by teenagers with their noise, vitality and truculence [belligerence] and, above all, their opinions.

These Students Are Not Inner City Youth

My comprehensive [school] is not in an inner city. Drink and drugs have appeared in the classroom but no knives. If Tess of the d'Urbervilles [title character of a novel by Thomas Hardy] were alive today she would probably be in my classroom (and still getting pregnant).

We are in an old-fashioned market town with its share of closed-down Zavvis [home entertainment chain]. Our children are a healthy mix of farm children bused in, children from rough council estates and the children of the newly "poor" middle classes.

When our children go truant they are either found drinking in the park or hiding in the cornfield. It is as fair a cross-section of society, neither one extreme or the other, as any school in the land.

Our nation has a shockingly high level of teenage pregnancies, but sometimes I feel that everything comes down to numbers and statistics, and the true stories behind the numbers are put aside. That, I suppose, is why I applied for the PSHE job.

I went into teaching because I love [English writers] Shakespeare and Elizabeth Barrett Browning and John Betjeman, not because I had any interest in teaching about cannabis and condoms; but somewhere along the line I realised that education is about a great deal more than one particular subject.

We have to send these children out as close to being whole people as possible, and that includes sometimes making up for whatever is missing elsewhere.

A Moment of Realisation

Perhaps the moment of truth for me [came] some years ago when I was trying to force an essay out of a girl who had suddenly given up working. She burst into tears and told me she could not concentrate on anything while she was so worried; she thought she was pregnant.

An hour later (going against every rule in the book) I was standing outside a lavatory cubicle reading Sarah the instructions on a pregnancy testing packet. I suspect I was praying as hard as she was while we waited for the blue lines. She was not pregnant. She hugged me and wept some more and thanked me. The next morning she brought me the essay.

A group of 14- to 15-year-old boys recently asked me if I thought they were "having sex". (It was in some way related to the text, but I was clearly being tested as to shockability.) I answered truthfully. Yes, I thought some of them were, most of them weren't, and all of them were thinking about it. But (because I am, after all, a teacher) now was not the moment to be thinking about it.

Not surprisingly boys are on the whole less discursive on such matters than girls. They'll shout rude things across the room, but they are unwilling to talk in anything more than smutty generalities. Girls, on the other hand, come to ask for advice. Particularly, I suspect, if they are not talked to very much at home.

The first thing is we should not think that all young teenagers are sexually active.

I walked into a classroom of girls once to be asked: "Miss, can I ask you something that's nothing to do with *Romeo and Juliet*"? When I told her yes, Marie said: "Is it all right if I don't sleep with my boyfriend? I don't want to yet, but they all say I'm being tight".

Her relief when I told her that it was certainly all right was almost palpable, and her dilemma turned into a general discussion within the classroom. I was flattered to be trusted in this conversation, but also curious to learn more about their attitudes.

Adults Should Not Assume All Teens Are Sexually Active

The first thing is, we should not think that all young teenagers are sexually active; many more aren't than are. It is hard to get a grip on actual figures as people lie in both directions—why shouldn't they? But it is the ones who are sexually active that are concerning.

I have heard horrific stories, from the children themselves, about how they carry on. Claire . . . needed the morning-after pill because after a "party" she had willingly lain down on a park bench and allowed four boys, one after the other, to have sex with her. "I just thought it was a laugh," she said, "but I'm scared now."

Jaydon . . . left home to live with her boyfriend and his father, fell out with the boyfriend and became pregnant by his father because she needed a place to stay. Sonia, in care, became pregnant, and her baby was taken away soon after birth with suspicious bruising. Sonia carries a picture of the baby around, sees her every day under supervision, but is not allowed to be alone with her.

I have heard of concerned mothers who, rather than suggest to their 14-year-old daughters that they wait a little longer to consummate their relationships, put candles around the child's bedroom, light joss sticks [incense], strew condoms on the pillow and leave their children to it.

A 13-year-old told me that her mother had made her have the contraceptive implant because "she knew I was having sex so she thought it was safer. I was consumed [conceived] against a fish and chip shop wall when she was 14, and she didn't want me to have a baby the same way".

That mother was one of the wise ones. While my school bucks both the national and local trends with its low level of pregnancies (ones that are allowed to go to term, at any rate), it is, time and again, the daughters of 15-year-olds who become mothers at 15. Our children, who leave us at 16, usually manage to wait before "consuming" their own babies, but some don't wait long. A few are born within a year.

[Teens] cut straight to the chase, skip the flirting and go straight to the bed.

All these stories point to the same assumption. It is all right to have sex—wiser to be protected from pregnancy, but perfectly all right to "shag". That's part of the problem—the carelessness of the vocabulary shows the carelessness of the undertaking of the act.

So when I was asked if I, as a teacher, was surprised by Alfie's story, I could only answer no. Not by Alfie, not by Chantelle Steadman, his "girlfriend" who was allegedly sleeping with more than five boys at the time her daughter Maisie was conceived, and not by the boys who have come forward to claim paternity.

I think we used to flirt with lots of boys when I was that age, but they don't flirt much now. They cut straight to the chase, skip the flirting and go straight to the bed. The Alfie story is shocking, of course. Surprising, alas not.

The Problem with PSHE and Sex Education

The non-statutory curriculum for PSHE says, of the sex and relationship component, that "it helps [students] to understand human sexuality and the significance of marriage and stable relationships as key building blocks of community and society".

Yet so much of PSHE ignores the latter half and focuses instead on how not to fall pregnant or catch a sexually transmitted infection. As one girl said to me recently: "Miss, they've been showing us how to put condoms on penises for years, but they never talk to us about relationships or how we choose." Out of the mouths of babes and sucklings.

The danger is that so much information is being blasted at these children on how not to conceive, where to go for help, the dangers of chlamydia, that the implied subtext is that it is all right to experiment with sex whenever you want. The curriculum does say that learning the advantages of delaying sexual activity should form part of the content, but how often is that touched upon?

I have formed a sex taskforce at my school, a group of teachers (all, interestingly, women) who have volunteered to be part of the sex education programme. We sat and stared blankly at a blue plastic penis while a school nurse trained us in condom use. We were told by the nurse that we were not to talk about flavoured condoms as we were not to imply that sex was for fun.

We were shown a little mat with a hole in to protect the boy/man giving cunnilingus (I wasn't the only one who hadn't heard of it before) and [told] where the children could pick one up. We were given femidoms [female condoms] and condoms and chlamydia testing kits and Lord knows what else, and by the end of the training hour I wondered what the children were going to be left thinking that sex was all about.

Trying to Get the Right Message Across

Is it a horrible, dangerous territory where the only way to proceed is to be wrapped in cling film from head to toe and hope for the best? Or is there any chance of emphasising that sex in the right context (which is clearly not on a park bench with four boys in a row) is a good thing one day, just maybe not yet?

Jason, a lazy, charming boy from year 11, came late into school the other day. He apologised, saying it was his turn to look after the baby while his girlfriend was at work. After a while he had decided to come into school anyway and had brought the baby with him. The baby was clean and sweet and had a much more expensive pram than anything any of my children slept in. I could not help but coo over the child and smile upon its child-father. . . .

What, to Jason, was the point of fatherhood? The pram as a show-off accessory? The baby as a conversation opener? Was it anything at all to do with looking after and loving and advising and guiding this boy through his first 18 years?

I seized on the second part of the general statement about sex and relationships education ("to understand . . . the significance of marriage and stable relationships as key building blocks of community and society") and designed a lesson on marriage. It was a good lesson. I taught it myself, and it generated thoughtful conversation about responsibility and parenthood and such like. But one of the PSHE teachers came to me and refused to teach it.

She said it made her "uncomfortable" and was "not relevant". I pointed out that "stable relationships" were to be emphasised as much as marriage; no one was to feel uncomfortable, that is the whole point of good PSHE. Still she refused. If parents don't, and teachers won't, teach children the basic tenets of moral responsibility, what chance do those children have?

Moral responsibility: these two words are the crux of the whole problem. Parents hold their hands up in despair; the government pushes the job back to the teachers, and no one ends up doing the job properly. No one will take moral responsibility, partly because the very word "moral" is frightening and threatening to a large proportion of our hedonistic, materialistic society, and partly because the "responsibility" always lies elsewhere.

How can we turn this around? As a mother I am infuriated when I receive letters from the government telling me how to avoid my children becoming obese. (Take exercise, eat healthy food, etc. Well, there's a thing.) I don't believe any parent in the land receives those letters and reads them seriously and highlights key phrases and uses them as a guideline. Of course not. So it is no good sending letters home about moral responsibility.

My fear is that we have a lost generation, but there is hope of a brighter future. Yes, we should be teaching these children how to avoid sexually transmitted diseases and pregnancies (and the dangers of drugs, etc.) but we should also be teaching them—or giving them, for this is something you cannot teach—self-respect.

Adults Should Be Leading by Example

We should be teaching them through example and conversation and mutual honesty (within reason) about the importance of family, not just as a system whereby we are given an annual holiday and a BMX [bicycle] and a computer. Somehow they need to be shown that there is a better way and [that] their own future families can be more whole than perhaps their present ones. . . . [If] families eat together and talk together and even argue together, they can communicate and understand each other better.

They say the English don't talk, especially about anything that matters, but my experience shows me that these children are only too willing to talk. Maybe that's where we should start—forget the condoms, and encourage the English to communicate, especially across the generations.

We are all, every one of us who complains about a corrupt society, capable of contributing to that. If you cross the road when you see a group of youths in hoodies, you are only reinforcing their isolation and their perception of themselves as some special pack. If we treat them as feral [wild], they become feral. And if they are already feral? Well, let's be optimistic. Most wild cats can be domesticated.

Teenage pregnancies are not a political problem; they are a problem of the society in which we live.

I have worked with bad and even mad children. I have worked with children with no home to speak of, or a home in which they are the prime carers. I have worked with truculent, downright aggressive and asocial teenagers. And I can tell you this: with some children it might take a very long time, with others it happens more quickly, but I don't believe there is a single child that will not respond to the simple technique of being talked to and listened to.

An Open and Honest Conversation with Teens Is Important

I have seen, in conversations with pupils, how they can learn from each other. One girl told me that her stepfather paid her a fiver a "moonie" [for baring her buttocks]. Another girl in the group, Sandra, who was not allowed to see her father unsupervised since he made her and her eight-year-old sister smoke a joint to quieten them down while he was looking after them, looked horrified and said: "That's not right, Ina. He shouldn't do that".

It was Sandra, not me, who made Ina question what was going on, who raised the subject of how families should or should not behave, but I enabled them to have the conversation without fear of ridicule. (On the other hand, the mooner is now 18 and pregnant with her second child by a second boy. Her mother has four children by three men. Go figure, as the Americans say.)

Teenage pregnancies are not a political problem; they are a problem of the society in which we live ... [a] society in which nobody, not even parents or teachers, can use words like "moral" without being scorned. That is why we teach children how to use condoms rather than how to say "no". Because if we cannot use a moral argument we have to use a practical one.

I remember talking to a group of 16-year-olds who were arguing that times had changed and now it was considered fine to sleep around. These are not 16-year-olds in a steady relationship, just ones out for a jolly on a Friday night.

They said (perfectly politely) that I was just old and out of the loop. So then I asked them this: would they like to think of their mothers as similar to the "fun-loving" girls they now associate with? Dared they imagine their mothers partying every night, drinking vodka, lying down in the park for a quick one?

I was met with a horrified silence, followed by a groan of disgust. Couldn't they see, I said, that one day they, too, would be parents, and did it not matter to them how their children would think of them?

I think that conversation had more impact than a million blue penises.

5

Parents Are Important in Influencing Teens' Sexual Behavior

Christine C. Kim

Christine C. Kim is policy analyst for the Heritage Foundation's Policy Studies Department.

The majority of teens who have sex regret their first sexual experience, but for many teens regret is not the only consequence. Among the consequences are teen pregnancy and sexually transmitted diseases. Health professionals, "safe sex" advocates, and others think that providing comprehensive sex education is the answer to teen sex issues; they are not taking into consideration the influence of parents on their teens' feelings and attitudes about sex, however. There are many different factors to this influence, including a stable family structure and parents' own values in regard to adolescent sex, with the most important being the strength of the relationship between the parent and the child. In light of this knowledge, parents should try to avoid sending mixed messages to their teens and work to strengthen their relationship with them.

The statistics on teen sexuality in the United States are troubling. About 7 percent of high school students report having had sex before the age of 13. By ninth grade, one-third of high school students have engaged in sexual activity, and by 12th grade, two-thirds. Yet the majority of these teens, 60 per-

Christine C. Kim, "Teen Sex: The Parent Factor," *Backgrounder*, October 7, 2008. Copyright © 2008 The Heritage Foundation. Reproduced by permission.

cent overall and 67 percent among younger adolescents, regret their first experience and wish they had waited longer. Sadly, for many teens, the consequences go far beyond regrets.

Teen Sexual Activity and Its Outcomes

Early sexual activity is associated with a host of negative outcomes that can have lasting physical, emotional, social, and economic impact on the lives of young people, particularly teenage girls and young women.

Engaging in early sexual activity elevates the risk of teenage girls becoming pregnant and single mothers.

Sexually Transmitted Diseases. The Centers for Disease Control and Prevention estimates that one in four teenage girls has at least one sexually transmitted infection (STI). Teenage girls, especially, are physiologically vulnerable to these infections, and early sexual activity increases the risk of infection. One study found that those who begin sexual activity at age 13 are twice as likely to become infected as peers who remain sexually abstinent throughout their teen years.

Teen Pregnancy and Unwed Childbearing. The National Campaign to Prevent Teen and Unplanned Pregnancy estimates that about one in two Hispanic and black teenage girls and one in five Caucasian teenage girls will become pregnant at least once before turning 20. Overall, nearly one in five adolescent girls will give birth in her teens.

Engaging in early sexual activity elevates the risk of teenage girls becoming pregnant and single mothers. Girls who become sexually active during early adolescence are three times as likely to become single mothers as those who remain abstinent throughout their teenage years. Nearly 40 percent of girls who begin sexual activity at ages 13 or 14 will give birth outside marriage, compared to 9 percent of those who remain abstinent until their early twenties.

Marital Stability and Maternal Poverty. Sexual activity at an early age may also affect marital and economic stability later in life. Among women in their thirties, those who were sexually active during early adolescence are half as likely to be in stable marriages as those who waited until their early twenties to have sex. Early sexual activity is also linked to maternal poverty. At the time of a large national survey in 1995, nearly 30 percent of mothers who began sexual activity at ages 13 or 14 lived in poverty compared to 12 percent of those who waited until their early twenties.

Parents . . . are the ones who have the most influence on their children's decisions about sex.

Parental Influence on Teen Sex

Many policymakers, health professionals, and "safe sex" advocates respond to these troubling statistics by demanding more comprehensive sex education and broader access to contraceptives for minors. They assume that teens are unable to delay their sexual behavior and that a combination of information about and access to contraceptives will effectively lead to protected sex, preventing any form of harm to youngsters. Not only are these assumptions faulty, they tend to disregard important factors that have been linked to reduced teen sexual activity. A particularly noticeable omission is parental influence.

Parents, as teens themselves reveal, are the ones who have the most influence on their children's decisions about sex. Indeed, two-thirds of all teens share their parents' values on this topic.

When it comes to talking about teen sex, both teens and parents report high levels of communication. Parents, however, tend to perceive a greater level of communication than do teens. Nearly all parents (90 percent) report having had a helpful conversation about delaying sex and avoiding pregnancy with their teenage children, compared to 71 percent of teens who report having had such a conversation with their parents. Many parents are also unaware of their teens' actual behavior. In a study of 700 teens in Philadelphia, 58 percent of the teens reported being sexually active, while only one-third of their mothers believed they were.

The empirical evidence on the association between parental influences and adolescents' sexual behavior is strong. Parental factors that appear to offer strong protection against the onset of early sexual activity include an intact family structure; parents' disapproval of adolescent sex; teens' sense of belonging to and satisfaction with their families; parental monitoring; and, to a lesser extent, parent-child communication about teen sex and its consequences.

That parents play a role in teen sex points to at least two significant policy implications. First, programs and policies that seek to delay sexual activity or to prevent teen pregnancy or STDs should encourage and strengthen family structure and parental involvement. Doing so may increase these efforts' overall effectiveness. Conversely, programs and policies that implicitly or explicitly discourage parental involvement, such as dispensing contraceptives to adolescents without parental consent or notice, contradict the weight of social science evidence and may prove to be counterproductive and potentially harmful to teens.

Research Finds Many Factors in Parental Influence

A Research Note. Social scientists are primarily concerned with the question of causality. For example, does parental disapproval of teen sex independently cause teens to delay sexual activity? Causality, however, is difficult to establish in social science research. Using statistical methods and appropriate data sources, social scientists infer certain reasonable conclusions from their research. The degree of confidence with which they draw inferred conclusions depends largely on data quality, study design, and statistical method.

The research on parental influences and teen sexuality is extensive. A substantial portion of the research is based on cross-sectional data, which capture information at one point in time and provide a "snapshot" view. As such, they limit researchers' ability to draw stronger conclusions. At best, cross-sectional data offer evidence of correlations, e.g., parental disapproval of teen sex is associated with delayed sexual initiation. Longitudinal surveys, on the other hand, follow the same group of individuals over time, which allows researchers to infer stronger findings. This paper mostly highlights findings from studies that use longitudinal data, which offer more rigorous conclusions.

Family Structure. A key parental influence on teen sex is family structure, for example, the number of parents living with, and their relationship to (biological, adoptive, step, or unrelated) the children in the families. The link between childhood family structure and the timing of sexual initiation has been well researched and documented. Research findings from studies that use a variety of data sources and that account for other factors associated with teen sexual behavior, such as gender, race and ethnicity, age, and family background, suggest the following:

- Adolescents living in intact families are more likely to delay sexual activity than peers living in other family forms. Parents' marital transitions, the absence of a natural father in the home, and the duration of such absences are significant as well.

- The protective influence of the intact family structure appears to vary by gender, age, and ethnicity, with stronger effects for adolescent girls, white teenagers, and younger teens.

- Teens living in intact families also tend to report fewer sexual experiences and partners, and are less likely to report being infected with a sexually transmitted disease, compared to peers in non-intact families. This is primarily because teens in intact families tend to delay sexual activity.

- Adolescent gifts in intact families are less likely to become pregnant and give birth outside of marriage compared to peers in non-intact families.

Yet, as sociologist Paul Amato notes, "[p]erhaps the most profound change in the American family over the past four decades has been the decline in the share of children growing up in households with both biological parents." In 1960, 88 percent of all children lived with two parents, compared to 68 percent in 2007. In 1960, 5 percent of all children born were to unmarried mothers. That figure rose to 38.5 percent in 2006. Thus, policies and programs that bolster the intact family structure and promote healthy marriages may reduce teen sexual activity.

Perceived parental disapproval of teen sex may also reduce the risk of teen pregnancy.

Parental Values and Disapproval of Teen Sex. Studies have demonstrated a robust correlation between parental values on teen sex and teen sexual behavior. Using longitudinal data, more recent research indicates that parental disapproval, particularly mothers' disapproval (fathers' values are less well studied), of their teens having sex appears to delay the onset of sexual activity. Importantly, the association is between teens' *perceptions* of their parents' disapproval, not necessarily parents' actual views, and delayed initiation. This does not mean that parental values are unimportant. In fact, research shows that, overall, parents' beliefs about teen sex are a significant predictor of teens' perceptions. (Another predictor appears to be strong parent-child relationships during early adolescence.)

Perceived parental disapproval of teen sex may also reduce the risk of teen pregnancy. The evidence suggests that adolescent girls tend to benefit more from this protective influence than do boys.

For example, in a study of 8,200 middle [school] and high school students nationwide, virgin teens who perceived stronger disapproval from their mothers during the baseline interview were less likely to have started sexual activity and report a pregnancy one year later than teens who viewed their mothers as having a more liberal attitude toward their engagement in sexual activity.

Studying younger and older teens together, as in the previous study, may bias the results, as older abstinent teens may have different characteristics than same-aged peers who are sexually experienced.

Another study, of younger adolescents ages 14 and 15, revealed similar findings, though the effect only appears statistically significant for girls. This relationship held true even considering adolescent girls' race, family structure, and dating history, as well as their mothers' education and religiosity, mothers' report of communication with their daughters on topics related to teen sex and birth control and of mother-daughter relationship quality, and the frequency of mothers' communication with the parents of their daughters' friends.

A third study, using longitudinal data, analyzed children ages 12 to 16 from the San Francisco Bay and the Los Angeles County areas, and found that perceived parental disapproval of teen sex also reduced the likelihood of teens engaging in oral sex one year later.

As noted earlier, parents and teens differ in their perceptions of the level of communication about teen sex issues and actual behavior that takes place. Thus, to ensure that teens perceive their parents' disapproval of teen sex accurately, parents should unequivocally convey their values to their teens. Mixed messages could potentially diminish any positive effects parental values have on delaying teen sexual behavior. In a national poll, teens were asked: "Suppose a parent or other adult tells you/a teen the following: 'Don't have sex, but if you do you should use birth control for protection.' Do you think this is a message that encourages you/teens to have sex?" One teen in two responded affirmatively, indicating that, to many teens, a qualified "no" translates into a perceived "yes."

Parent-Child Relationships. A third robust protective parental element is strong parent-child relationships. Parent-child relationship quality or connectedness is often measured by the level of satisfaction teens and their parents experience in their relationships with one another; the amount of warmth, love, affection, and communication teens report receiving from their parents; and the level of parental involvement in their children's lives. In a thorough review of the research on family relationships and teen pregnancy risk published before 2000, Dr. Brent Miller and colleagues write:

> There is marked consistency in this body of more than 20 studies . . . all but a few indicate that parent/child closeness is associated with reduced adolescent pregnancy risk through teens remaining sexually abstinent, postponing intercourse, having fewer sexual partners, or using contraception more consistently.

Four recent longitudinal studies, analyzing the same nationally representative survey of students in grades seven through eleven across the nation, report the following:

Teens who reported greater satisfaction in their relationships with their mothers were less likely to have sex and become pregnant (and were also more likely to use birth control during their most recent sexual experience) one year later than peers who felt less satisfied in their relationships with their mothers.

Fourteen- and fifteen-year-old adolescent girls whose mothers reported greater satisfaction in their relationships with their teens were less likely to initiate sexual activity one year later than peers of mothers who felt less satisfied in their relationships with their daughters.

For teenage girls, but not for boys, higher quality *father-daughter* relationships, but not mother-daughter relationships, tended to postpone sexual activity. This connection appeared to be explained by the observation that adolescent girls who have better relationships with their fathers also have fewer dating relationships, associate more guilt with having sex, and share more meals with their parents relative to peers who reported lower-quality father-daughter relationships.

Younger teenage girls and boys as well as older teenage boys who felt more connected to their mothers tended to delay sexual activity compared to similar-age peers who felt less connected to their mothers.

Parental Monitoring and Parenting Practices. Most research on parental monitoring—for example, the extent to which parents know the whereabouts and activities of their children outside home and school—parental supervision, and parental rules shows a positive correlation between these factors and reduced teen sexual activity. For studies that do not demonstrate such a relationship, Dr. Miller posits that "excessive or coercive" parental control might actually lead to negative outcomes. The following findings come from several recent longitudinal studies:

In a study of some 750 children ages 13 and older, adolescents who received more parental monitoring were more likely to delay sexual initiation one year later compared to peers who received less monitoring from their parents. This applied to dating teens as well. However, teen sexual behavior appeared uninfluenced by parenting style, either supportive (characterized by frequently praising and spending time with the child) or coercive (characterized by spanking, yelling, or arguing with the child) parenting.

In a study of nearly 900 youths, ages 12 to 16, from the San Francisco Bay and Los Angeles County areas, those who reported more parental monitoring or those whose parents limited their television were less likely to engage in oral sex one year later, compared to peers whose parents were less knowledgeable about their whereabouts outside school and home or whose parents did not limit their television viewing. While parental monitoring was not associated with sexual initiation in this study, parental limitations on and co-viewing of television appeared to be associated with delayed sexual initiation.

In a study of young minority adolescent boys from low-income areas of Chicago, Boston, and San Antonio, those who reported greater levels of parental monitoring were less likely to initiate sexual activity before age 15 compared to peers who received less parental monitoring. Parental monitoring also had an indirect influence on engaging in risky sexual behavior through reduced substance use and school problems.

In a cross-sectional sample of black female adolescents ages 14 and 18, parental monitoring was related to a reduction in testing positive for STDs.

Parent-Child Communication. The evidence on parent-child communication, particularly communication about sex and birth control, is more mixed. Reviewing 30 studies published before 2000, Dr. Brent Miller and colleagues summarize the research as follows:

> Results across these studies are complex and discrepant. Perhaps the clearest conclusion that can be drawn from these studies is that there is no simple direct effect. That is, parent-teen communication about sexual issues has no uniform or consistent effect on adolescent pregnancy risk that holds

across gender, race, source of data (parent or child report), and especially across parental attitudes and values.

While some studies have reported an inverse correlation between communication and teen sexual activity—more communication, less teen sexual activity—others have reported a positive association—more communication, more teen sexual activity. Neither relationship should be interpreted as causal (for example, communication causes teens to engage in sexual activity). Still other studies have reported no significant correlations. The following studies present some of the mixed results:

In a study of teens ages 12 to 16 from the San Francisco Bay and Los Angeles County areas, the teens were asked about the quality of their general communication with their parents as well as whether they and their parents had talked about sex-related topics in the past year. Teens who reported better quality communication with their mothers were less likely to engage in oral sex one year later. General father-teen communication did not appear to affect teen oral sex, nor did general parent-child communication appear to have an effect on sexual initiation. However, teens who talked with their parents about sexual issues in the past year were *more* likely to engage in oral sex and sexual activity compared to peers who did not have such discussions.

A study of some 200 adolescents and young adults from Madison, Wisconsin, found that general parent-child communication appeared to delay sexual activity over time.

Two longitudinal studies of a national representative survey of teens—one examining younger adolescents, . . . the other, eighth- through eleventh-graders—did not find any direct links between mother-teen communication about sex-related topics and teen sexual behavior. When mothers recommended a specific type of birth control to their teens, however, teens tended to perceive less disapproval from their mothers regarding teen sex, which, in turn, appeared to have an encouraging effect on initiating sexual activity.

Interestingly, one cross-sectional study of some 600 middle school students from the South Bronx in New York City found that when mothers talked to their teens about the moral and social consequences of early sexual activity, teens were more likely to delay sexual initiation. Talking about the physical and health risks associated with early sexual activity did not appear to affect teens' behavior.

Clearly, the research on parental influences and teen sexual behavior is rich and nuanced. A few broad trends emerge:

- The intact family structure is associated with delayed and reduced levels of teen sexual activity and reduced risk of teen pregnancy.

- Parental disapproval of teen sex, specifically teens' perceptions of their mothers' disapproval, is linked to delayed sexual activity and reduced risk of teen pregnancy

- Higher levels of parent-teen relationship satisfaction and a strong connection between teens and their mothers are associated with delayed sexual initiation.

- Greater parental monitoring and rules appear to be correlated with reduced teen sexual activity, though the evidence is mixed.

- The evidence on parent-child communication, in general or specifically about sexual issues, is mixed. Here, the relationship may vary by the content and degree of discussion as well as other factors.

What Parents Should Do

From a parent's perspective, the implications are clear: Parents can, in fact, influence their children's sexual behavior and offer protection against the negative consequences of early sexual activity. The two strongest links appear to be parental values regarding teen sex and parents' relationships with their children. Consequently, parents should:

- Avoid sending ambiguous and mixed messages about teen sex;

- Convey clearly to their teens their values on this subject;

- Focus on imparting clearly defined values—simply discussing sex, contraceptives, and physiology does not necessarily protect teens; and

- Seek to strengthen their relationships with their teenage children.

Policies that discourage parental involvement . . . contradict the weight of social science evidence and should be opposed.

What Policymakers Should Do

From a policy perspective, the implications are clear as well: Parents can influence teen sexual behavior and related outcomes. Policymakers should:

- Include a component on healthy marriage, stable family formation, and parental involvement in programs and policies that seek to delay teen sexual activity or prevent teen-sex related negative outcomes.

- Oppose programs and policies that discourage parental involvement. For example, policies that dispense contraceptives to teens, in school-based clinics and other settings, without parental consent or notification are clearly contrary to the weight of social science evidence and might weaken a demonstrated protective influence against early teen sexual activity and related outcomes.

- Endorse programs and policies that promote strong marriage and stable family formation.

Parents Play a Protective Role

Nationally, a non-trivial portion of teens engage in sexual activity before the age of 13. By ninth grade, one teen in three has had sex, and by twelfth grade, two in three. Early sexual activity is associated with a host of enduring negative consequences that include increased risks of psychological and physical harm, teen pregnancy and unwed childbearing, poverty, and marital instability later in life.

Social science research over the decades suggests that parents can play a protective role in delaying early teen sexual activity and reducing the risk of harmful consequences. Importantly, the empirical evidence indicates that childhood family structure, teens' perceptions of parental disapproval of teen sex, and the quality of the parent-child relationship appear to affect teen sexual behavior. The evidence on parental monitoring and parent-child communication, in general and specifically about sex-related topics, appears more mixed.

Consequently, programs and policies focused on reducing teen sexual activity and [its] damaging results should encourage parents' presence and involvement in the lives of their children. Policies that discourage parental involvement, such as dispensing contraceptives to teens without parental consent, contradict the weight of social science evidence and should be opposed.

6

Teens Are Using Abortions as Contraception

Beverly Kemp and Claie Wilson

Beverly Kemp is a journalist who contributes frequently to News of the World *as well as* The Independent *and* The Times. *Claie Wilson is also a journalist and a feature writer for* News of the World.

Even though sex education is increasing in the schools of the United Kingdom teen pregnancies are still on the rise, as is the number of abortions these teens are receiving. What is especially disturbing about this development is the fact that these pregnant teens are repeatedly getting pregnant and repeatedly receiving abortions as a form of birth control. Just having one abortion can lower a teen's chances of being able to conceive when she is actually ready, but having multiple abortions can take a serious toll on her body. Not only is a teen physically scarred by abortions, but the procedures have extremely damaging emotional effects as well, proving that abortions should not be used as a form of birth control.

The silence of the stark hospital room was broken by the ticking of a clock hanging on the wall opposite her bed— and the violent sobs that shook Mandy Brown. She'd just had a termination—her third in as many years. But this was the first time she'd cried, because she blamed herself.

"I was consumed by feelings of anger and sadness," she says. "Before, I could tell myself that I'd been young and stupid, but at 18 I should have known better. I felt an over-whelming grief for the baby whose life I had just terminated."

Teen Pregnancy Is Still Rising

Mandy, now 19, is just one of the tens of thousands of teen-agers in the UK who have abortions to end unwanted preg-nancies each year. Despite increased sex education within schools, the number of teen pregnancies continues to rise and, more worryingly, at least 100 teenagers a month are having an abortion for the second time.

Last year [in 2008] there were 195,296 NHS [National Health Service] abortions in England and Wales—41,593 were performed on girls aged 15–19. And a new survey of teenagers across the UK for *Fabulous* [Magazine] showed that 38 per cent of those who had abortions had not used any contracep-tion.

Kitty Hagenbach, psychotherapist at the Viveka clinic, which specialises in women and children's health, says: "While we would never want to go back to the days of backstreet abortions, today's quick-fix culture means that many young girls see abortion as just another form of contraception. It's easy to get the morning-after or abortion pill, which also in-creases their relaxed attitude towards sex."

At least 100 teenagers a month are having an abortion for the second time.

Peer Pressure Is Not Helping

Meanwhile, peer pressure and the rise of under-age drinking only adds to the problem.

Fabulous GP [general practitioner] Dr Hilary Jones says the increase in teen terminations is worrying. "There's clearly huge pressure for young and immature people to have sex be-fore they're physically or psychologically ready," he says. "The tragedy is that these traumatic procedures are avoidable, and have far-reaching consequences—from guilt, to regret, to fertility problems later in life."

One Girl's Story

Finance assistant and part-time model Mandy, from Yorkshire, admits that when she first became pregnant—aged 15—she hadn't used contraception. Like many teens, she thought she wouldn't get pregnant.

But she did. And on her 16th birthday she underwent her first abortion at an NHS clinic.

"It sounds selfish, but I wasn't prepared to let anything get in the way of the modelling career I'd always dreamed of. I wouldn't have been able to look after a baby financially or emotionally," she admits.

Mandy kept her pregnancy secret—she was embarrassed and worried about being branded a "slag [prostitute]". When she told her then boyfriend, he shrugged off any responsibility, saying the pregnancy was "her problem" and dumped her. In desperation, Mandy called an aunt, who accompanied her to a clinic for a termination. "I kept holding my tummy and saying: 'I'm sorry.' I never thought I would find myself in that situation," she says.

The procedure was routine, but she bled heavily afterwards and was kept in hospital overnight. Her mother thought she was at a friend's for a sleepover.

"The next day, I was discharged but I couldn't bring myself to go straight home—I didn't want to face Mum. I went to the local park and sat on the swings thinking: 'You idiot, what have you done?'" she says.

A year later, Mandy underwent another termination. Although she was on the Pill, she often forgot to take it. She missed two periods and a test confirmed she was pregnant. She told her boyfriend, Dean McDonald, 19, and they agreed she should have a termination.

"Until then, he hadn't known about my first abortion, but I ended up breaking down and telling him," Mandy says quietly. "He shouted at me for being so irresponsible and walked out the room, although he came back to apologise and gave me a cuddle."

"I'd just got a modelling contract worth £10,000. I wasn't going to lose it by telling them I was pregnant. I pushed the fact that I had another child growing inside me to the back of my mind."

Two weeks later, she was back at the clinic having her second abortion. This time she was on her own—Dean was on holiday with his friends and no one else knew.

A couple of hours after the procedure, Mandy was allowed home. Dean texted her to see if she was OK. She recovered quickly and was back modelling within 24 hours.

"If, as a teen, you aren't prepared to talk about sex and contraception, you're not ready to have sex."

After the trauma of the termination, you'd think Mandy would be ultra-cautious with contraception. But just a year later, she fell pregnant again—aged 18. Although she'd been taking the Pill regularly, she'd been on antibiotics for a chest infection, which had reduced the Pill's effectiveness. Weeks later the familiar feelings of pregnancy washed over her— nausea, dizziness, and bloating. She did a home test, then rang her GP and booked in for another termination.

"The nurse at the clinic, who'd been so reassuring the first time, looked at me with disbelief," reveals Mandy. "She explained that having three abortions in three years was dangerous and could affect my future fertility. She tried to persuade me to have a contraceptive implant, but I refused because I'd heard they can make you put on weight. As a model, that's the last thing I want."

Yet again, she had a termination. This time, Dean was with her. "It took me weeks to stop crying," she says. "But I knew I'd resent being tied down. If I had a baby, I wouldn't have time to model and earn money. I left school at 16 and am not qualified to do any other job. People may think I'm selfish, but I think it's selfish to bring a baby into this world unless you have the time to be the best possible mother."

Dr Hilary says: "The fact teens have multiple abortions means parents, sex educators and health-care professionals are letting them down. But if, as a teen, you aren't prepared to talk about sex and contraception, you're not ready to have sex."

Now Mandy takes the Pill daily but worries she may struggle to have the family she wants one day.

"Part of me does feel ashamed, but I know I made the right decision," she says. "I hope one day I'll be in a position to be the good mum I wouldn't have been as a teenager."

Abortions Can Leave Teens Emotionally Scarred

Nia Valentine, 21, from London, is a business and law student at Kingston University. She's had two abortions and has used the morning-after pill 10 times.

"I started having sex at 16 but never gave much thought to contraception. We weren't told a lot at school, and some of my friends had been through abortions and didn't seem too affected by it, so I saw it as an option if I did get pregnant. Which is why, at the age of 17, I had a termination.

"I met my boyfriend Jimmy at school. He always wanted unprotected sex because he said it was nicer for him. On his 17th birthday, I caved in and agreed. I told myself I'd just take the morning-after pill. I'd already used it twice when condoms split—it was just like taking a sweet as far as I was concerned. But it was the weekend, and the clinic was shut. It was another two days before I was able to take it, but I never thought it might not work. My periods were always irregular, so when I missed one I didn't worry. By the time I suspected anything and booked a doctor's appointment, I was nine weeks pregnant. Stupidly I was delighted, but Jimmy was furious. I realised I was too young, so three weeks later, I had a termination.

"Afterwards, Jimmy took me home and tucked me into bed. I cried for a week. I wasn't in any physical pain, I just hurt inside. Eventually I told my mum, who was brilliant. She told me I had to be more careful, and took me to the family-planning clinic to pick up some leaflets about birth control, but I didn't want to go on the Pill as I thought I'd forget to take it.

Abortion is not something that should be taken lightly.

"Jimmy and I split when I was 19—our relationship never recovered from the abortion. A month later I met Sam, who was four years older than me. I wanted to make him happy, and when he insisted on unprotected sex, I stupidly agreed. Sam told me he would pull out before he ejaculated, and I knew I could take the morning-after pill if anything went wrong. Of course Sam didn't keep his promise, and I ended up taking the morning-after pill seven times in a year. I went to different clinics so no one would ask me any questions. But in November 2007 I became pregnant. I knew straight away I wanted an abortion as I didn't see a long-term future with Sam. This time, I decided on the abortion pill as I was only seven weeks gone, and I'd hated being under anaesthetic. The night before I was due to take the second of the two pills, Sam and I had a massive row because he didn't want me to go through with it, and we split up, so I had to turn to my mum again. She was furious but came to the hospital with me to get the pill.

"A couple of hours after taking it, I began to bleed heavily and was in excruciating pain. Half an hour later, I was on the toilet weeping and doubled over with pain as my baby was aborted. Emotionally, I felt heavy with guilt, while the bleeding carried on for four weeks.

"It's a year and a half since my second abortion and I still can't get the horrific memories out of my head. I haven't had sex since—I don't want to. I bitterly regret how careless I was. Abortion is not something that should be taken lightly, and I've had to learn that the hard way."

7

Teen Abortion Rates Are Declining

Sarah Kliff

Sarah Kliff is a writer for Newsweek.

As abortion rates have steadily decreased over the years, the de-mographic has changed as well. Even though pop culture would indicate otherwise, teens are not the ones getting abortions. It is the older, twenty-something population that is making up the biggest percentage, which has increased ten points since 1974. Researchers feel that the reason for these unwanted pregnancies among the older generation is due to programs focusing on teens, and not this older age group, because teens seem more vulner-able. Another reason is that this age group doesn't have health insurance, which hinders access to birth control. There are many factors in these women's decisions to have these abortions, one of the most important of which is financial strain.

Abortion rates have dropped steadily since the 1980s, from a peak of 29.3 abortions per 1,000 women in 1981 to 19.4 in 2005. But behind this general decrease are striking changes in the demographics of abortion. Compared to 30 years ago, women having abortions today are older and more likely to be mothers and minorities, according to a study released Tuesday [September 16, 2008] by the nonprofit, non-partisan Guttmacher Institute.

Teens Are Not the Ones Getting Abortions

The study looked at trends in abortion since 1974, the year after the Supreme Court passed *Roe v. Wade*, legalizing abortion in the United States. What researchers found is contrary to what pop culture . . . from [the title character of the movie] *Juno* to Jamie Lynn Spears, might suggest: Teenagers are not the most likely to confront this issue; twenty-somethings are. "We're aware that, today, most of the women having abortions are moms struggling to take care of the children they already have," says Rachel Jones, senior research associate at the institute.

In fact, teens saw a bigger drop in abortion rates than any other demographic over the past 30 years. From 1974 to 1989, women [ages] 18–19 had the highest abortion rate among all age groups, varying from 32 to 62 per 1,000 women. In 2004, the latest year for which data is available, the abortion rate [for that age group] was 20.5. "We've done a great job educating kids about the risks of sexual behavior and proper contraceptive use," says Jones. So it's not the kids that researchers are most worried about—it's the age groups above them.

The Bad Side of the Statistics

But the news isn't all good. While the teen abortion rate has declined by nearly 30 percent, the rate for women ages 20–24 is almost 10 points higher than it was in 1974. (In that group, rates hit 30.4 abortions per 1,000 women in 1974, spiking to 53.8 in 1989 and declining to 39.9 in 2004.) Women in the next age group, ages 25–29, follow a similar pattern, with a spike in the 1980s and a decline in recent years. So while it's encouraging that abortion rates among 20- to 29-year-olds have been steadily declining since the late 1980s, those decreases have been much smaller than those among teenagers, and they still have not brought the abortion rate down to [the] low levels of the 1970s.

Researchers cannot fully explain the reasons behind this trend. Some think it indicates a kind of oversight: Public health initiatives have focused on reducing pregnancy and abortions among teenagers but haven't put as much thought into how to educate older groups. Teenagers, after all, do seem like the most vulnerable group. Millions of dollars have been poured into programs to educate teenagers about safe sex and contraceptives. By most accounts, those efforts have been fairly successful in targeting and changing the sexual health habits of teens. Centers for Disease Control [and Prevention] statistics show teenage contraceptive use to have gone up noticeably between 1995 and 2005. The decline in abortion rates among teens mirrors a decline in teen pregnancies—from 107 for every 1,000 teenagers ages 15–19 in 1982, to 75 per 1,000 teenagers in 2002 (the most recent year for which data is available).

Financial barriers seem to be one of the most persistent obstacles in the fight to reduce socioeconomic disparities in abortion rates.

Lack of Health Insurance Is to Blame

But once they're out of high school and on their own, many women don't have an adequate support system when it comes to reproductive health. "We've done a lot for adolescents and teens but need to expand those efforts to reach adult women," says Jones. "We haven't taken care of women in their 20s." Experts say a lack of health insurance, more common among adults than teens, and access to affordable contraceptives are significant factors in causing abortion rates to stay at a level higher than that of the 1970s among older women. "You could full-well know that the pill or IUDs are effective [birth control], but if you don't have health insurance or don't have access to affordable family planning, that's not going to help you much," says Jones.

Financial barriers seem to be one of the most persistent obstacles in the fight to reduce socioeconomic disparities in abortion rates, say experts. Medicaid coverage of birth control varies by state, and the bureaucracy can be difficult to navigate. The current Guttmacher study did not look at the socioeconomic status of women having abortions, but the institute's previous research has shown the abortion rates for women below the federal poverty line to be much higher than for more economically advantaged women. "When you don't have access to affordable birth control, rates of unintended pregnancy are going to be higher. That's a sad and real-life consequence of the health insurance gap," says Laurie Rubiner, Planned Parenthood's vice president of public policy.

Women Are Having Abortions Because of Financial Strain

Other shifts in demographics bolster Rubiner's claim that the women having abortions today are increasingly under economic duress: Compared with 1974, they are much more likely to already have children, as well as to be unmarried. "Women are making a decision, 'Can I feed another mouth,'" says Kim Gandy, president of the National Organization of Women. "'Did my husband leave me with three other kids? Is this going to mean that I can't feed my kids?' There is a real life decision that a woman has to make." Many women, she thinks, are asking whether they can afford to have another child.

Another trend uncovered by the study that Planned Parenthood's Rubiner finds troubling is the consistently higher rate of abortion among minority women. While the abortion rates among African Americans and Hispanics have decreased since 1994 (the first year for which ethnic data is available), they are still dramatically higher than those of Caucasian women. The abortion rate for black women is 49.7 per 1,000 women, nearly five times that of non-Hispanic white women.

These sobering numbers leave reproductive health experts looking ahead to a whole new set of challenges even as they celebrate the significant strides they've made in the past 30 years. Closing a socioeconomic health-care gap decades in the making won't be easy.

8

Teens Have Casual Attitudes About Oral Sex

Debra Jopson and Elicia Murray

Debra Jopson has been a news reporter, feature writer and editor for several newspapers, including The Sydney Morning Herald *and the* Brisbane Times. *Elicia Murray is the urban affairs reporter for the* Sydney Morning Herald.

If Australian adults actually knew the sexual activity of Australian teenagers, they would be appalled. More sexually experienced than their parents were at their age, these teens' favorite pastimes are drinking and having sex parties. At many of these parties the boys line up to receive oral sex from the girls, who don't consider it as big a deal as actually having intercourse and losing their virginity. In this time of sexual promiscuity, however, there are still teens who choose to remain virgins because they know many other teens who have regretted having sex.

In a week of public outrage at footballers' sexual behaviour, Debra Jopson and Elicia Murray found that past taboos are, for some, the new norm.

Any Saturday night, teenagers are doing it in the dark places—parks, garages, backyards, beaches, schools, the backs of cars. Partying, drinking, drugs and sex, even in trees, according to 17-year-old Tania, who lost her virginity at 13.

She knows of a girl, 15, and her 14-year-old male lover who had sex in a tree in a park because lying on the grass made them itchy. "My advice to everyone is they should not walk through a park on a Saturday night or a teenager might fall on their head," says Tania.

The Matthew Johns [group sex] scandal, involving Cronulla rugby league players and a woman, 19, in Christchurch, New Zealand, seven years ago, [in 2002] has lifted the lid on moral outrage and raised deep questions about consent, power, vulnerability and responsibility. The footballers are required to atone, and the woman's behaviour in apparently giving at least limited consent remains a sad puzzle to many.

Shocked as older Australians may be at those sordid details, however, events under their noses are more likely to shake them. Many teenagers and young adults have turned the free-sex mantra of the 1970s into a lifestyle, and older generations simply don't have a clue.

Teens Are Far More Advanced than Their Parents Were

Group sex may still be fringe, but a fair proportion of sexually active teenagers and young adults interviewed last week have been involved in threesomes, or know of friends who have.

Oral sex is no longer the exotic addition to the normal repertoire of their parents' generation. For the young who do sex, oral is the norm. For them, it's the equivalent of their parents snogging during courtship. They get pornography, advice and pick-ups over the internet, and alcopops [flavored Alcoholic Beverages], which appeal to younger women drinkers, evaporate inhibitions.

Many teenagers and young adults have turned the free-sex mantra of the 1970s into a lifestyle.

"I've had threesomes and foursomes," says Lisa, 19. "It's usually at a party, and everyone's had a bit to drink. It started with girls kissing girls because that's a hot thing. After that you're just kissing everyone, and it goes on from there."

Not that everyone is doing it, of course. The national Secondary Students and Sexual Health survey in 2002 found that a quarter of year 10 students and half of year 12 students were no longer virgins. Half of school leavers, therefore, had not had intercourse. The La Trobe University researchers say the unreleased 2009 results are similar, with only a slight shift to permissiveness.

But among the sexually active, stories abound of games at the edge, like "lipstick parties", also known as rainbow parties. "The girls all wear a different shade of lipstick," says a high-school teacher at a school where a female student was caught trying to organise one such party.

Young females have become more brazen; males less inhibited.

"Guys have to get as many shades as possible on their dicks. The girls will line up on their knees and the guys will go around the group getting different coloured rings so it looks like a rainbow on their dicks," [she says]

Moral judgements will no doubt be made about what many of the young now get up to, but listening to their voices tells a different sexual story to that of previous generations.

Oral Sex Is No Longer a Big Deal

The age of first sex has fallen since the 1960s. Young females have become more brazen; males less inhibited. The history of this is based on the behaviour of their elders.

"It is not a clock we can turn back," says Anne Mitchell, associate professor at La Trobe University's Australian Research Centre for Sex, Health and Society.

There has been a gradual shift in sexual culture towards permissiveness since the contraceptive pill first wrought a revolution in the 1960s and 1970s, when Mitchell was a young adult.

"That is when the gap between puberty and marriage started to grow. In the past you got married to start a sex life. The pill was huge. It made the difference between the shame of having a baby out of wedlock (and not) . . . The gap between puberty and marriage means there is a lot of territory where you cannot expect everyone to be [abstinent]," says Mitchell.

"When we were young, oral sex was part of your fantasy sex agenda. For young people now it is foreplay. They don't consider oral sex as sex."

Eve, 19, says most of her friends were about 16 when they started having sexual intercourse, years after their first experience of oral sex. "People were talking about it and doing it in year 7," she says.

For girls, she says, there is not the same stigma attached to oral sex as there is to intercourse. "It's a big thing with losing their virginity. They have to wait. But with oral sex, it's like whatever. It's normal."

Wendy Delaney, a teachers' union representative who works as a school counsellor in the Newcastle area of NSW [New South Wales], said she knew of several cases of year 6 students having oral sex. All were reported to the Department of Community Services.

Even Now a Double Standard Still Applies

Eve has been to parties where guys lined up for oral sex. A double standard can apply.

"For the guys, there's a hero status. But for the girls, most of the other girls will look at them and think it's a bit slutty. But most of them are so drunk that they don't know what they're doing anyway," she says.

Young women's behaviour shifted during the 1990s as they "became more like the men"—more open about what they had done with their partners, eroding the double standard, says Juliet Richters, associate professor in sexual health at the University of [New South Wales].

In surveys of university students at Macquarie [University] during the 1990s, she found that men lost the 1960s perception of themselves as creatures driven by sexual urges who needed females to control them.

As sexual practices changed, language evolved. Terms such as "friend with benefits", "f--- buddy" or "bed buddy" are used to describe someone who is a no-strings-attached regular sexual partner. Encounters are known as "hook-ups" and "booty calls".

Lisa, 19, has two such friends. "We just have sex every time we see each other. There's no jealousy," she says. "Free love, man, free love."

Some Virgins Are Standing Their Ground

In this atmosphere, are virgins intimidated? Says Mitchell: "There is still a large number of young people who haven't had sex or even a bit of snogging. We know 20 per cent of young people in the school survey haven't had any kind of sexual contact." Richters says the virgins she surveyed at university "were always amazed because they always think that everyone has had it except them". Brazen they may be, but many young people regret the circumstances of their loss of virginity.

"I should have waited till I was older and more mature," says Tania, who had sex with a boyfriend at 13.

Joan Sauers' *Sex Lives of Teenagers* tells many tales of joy, regret and alcohol. "Well, I was really, really drunk and I had a boyfriend, but I went to a party and was with three guys," says a West Australian, who lost her virginity at 15. "It felt really good at the time, but afterwards I felt cheated and used."

Tania says some in her group use fake IDs to get into pubs. That's preferable, she says, to the dark spaces where they otherwise party, because kids made adventurous by drink tend to do more stupid things, like going naked.

Her friends have combined ecstasy and alcohol and ended up having unwanted sex. The secondary schools survey found an increase in alcohol use and bingeing between 1997 and 2002. More than 28 per cent of girls and 23 per cent of boys reported having unwanted sex in 2002.

Mitchell says "alcopops have had an enormous impact on young women" who previously didn't drink because there was no respectable beverage.

Lara, 19, says group sex—usually spur of the moment and alcohol-fuelled—is common at her university residences, where she has heard of anything from threesomes to encounters with up to a dozen people.

Pride can turn to shame once their exploits become public knowledge.

"It's the whole dorm-living thing. It goes on a whole lot," she says. "Group sex is mainly involving three guys and a girl, but I have heard of up to nine or 10 guys and two girls . . . All scenarios are pretty much imaginable."

Lara says that while some women students enjoy the physical act, others find the attention more appealing. "I honestly think that some of the girls do it because the guys will think they're amazing," she says.

But pride can turn to shame once their exploits become public knowledge. "You'll notice a complete turnaround within a week or two, based on what's circulating about them," says Lara.

Trent, 21, says he has high-fived a mate during group sex but tries to keep emotions out of it. "I don't really want the girl to get too emotionally involved," he says.

"Sexting" Can Be Just as Bad

Sex these days is even possible without being there, thanks to "sexting." The NSW Government launched an education campaign this month to warn children about the dangers of sending sexual images via mobile phone or posting pictures on social networking sites.

Chris, 16, likens it to fishing: "You chuck a line out and see if anything bites," he says. Lisa describes the practice as "like a gift to whoever you're going out with." But it has to be "artistic." "Not like 'Here is a vagina.' That's pretty gross," she says. But she acknowledges that it doesn't always end well. "They'll just forward it to their mates if they're a dickhead. You've got to be careful."

Girls also collect photos of themselves having sex with as many different partners as they can, says Lara. Tom, 17, says a stash of porno mags under the bed is "old generation". He accesses pornography online. There's plenty of it, and it's free. Chris has been downloading videos to his mobile phone for years. He was caught out by a relative when a huge phone bill arrived, but that has not deterred him.

Teens Are Learning from Others' Mistakes

Tania says she and her friends talk about the right and wrong of what they do. "We learn morals from other people's experiences," she says.

According to Mitchell, now that many sexual roles have gone, young people can develop personal ethics. "We need to understand that kids will have sex when they are not married," she says. "Our concern would be to make them safe and enjoy it."

9

Abstaining Teens Are Not Replacing Sex with Oral Sex

Rob Stein

Rob Stein is a staff writer for The Washington Post.

In the first national study done on the topic, researchers have found that teens who are abstinent are not having oral sex in place of intercourse, disproving the myth that says otherwise. Although many teens admitted to having engaged in oral sex, they had also engaged in actual intercourse. Many supporters of abstinence education say that this study only reinforces the need for the programs, while critics say it proves the need for increased comprehensive sex education. Also, sixty-seven percent of all teens surveyed reported having only one partner, adding to the evidence that teens are not engaging in what is known as "serial oral sex," disproving the hype about oral sex parties.

Contrary to widespread belief, teenagers do not appear to commonly engage in oral sex as a way to preserve their virginity, according to the first study to examine the question nationally.

The analysis of a federal survey of more than 2,200 males and females aged 15 to 19, released yesterday, [May 19, 2008.] found that more than half reported having had oral sex. But those who described themselves as virgins were far less likely to say they had tried it than those who had had intercourse.

"There's a popular perception that teens are engaging in serial oral sex as a strategy to avoid vaginal intercourse," said Rachel Jones of the Guttmacher Institute, a private, nonprofit research organization based in New York, who helped do the study. "Our research suggests that's a misperception."

Teens Have Oral and Vaginal Sex at About the Same Time

Instead, the study found that teens tend to become sexually active in many ways at about the same time. For example, although only one in four teenage virgins had engaged in oral sex, within six months after their first intercourse more than four out of five adolescents reported having oral sex.

"That suggests that oral and vaginal sex are closely linked," said Jones, whose findings will be published in the July [2008] issue of the *Journal of Adolescent Health*. "Most teens don't have oral sex until they have had vaginal sex."

Proponents of sex-education programs that focus on abstinence said the findings debunked the criticism that the approach was inadvertently prompting more teens to have oral sex, which still carries the risk of sexually transmitted disease, in order to preserve their virginity.

Teens tend to become sexually active in many ways at about the same time.

"This study . . . invalidates the suggestion that 'technical virgins' account for the rise in oral and anal sex," said Valerie Huber, executive director of the National Abstinence Education Association. "Sexually experienced teens were almost four times more likely to engage in oral sex and 20 times more likely to engage in anal sex than their peers who were virgins."

If anything, the findings support the need to encourage more teens to delay sexual activity of all kinds, she said.

Fueling the Debate over Abstinence or Comprehensive Sex Education

"This report reveals that teen sex—even with a condom—presents significant risk for future sexual experimentation and so underscores the need for redoubled emphasis on abstinence education for teens," she said. "Only abstinence education adequately addresses this problem."

But critics of abstinence programs said the findings reinforced the need for comprehensive sex education, because teens engage in a wide variety of sexual activities, all of which can spread sexually transmitted diseases.

"More than half of our teens are having sex—vaginal and oral," said James Wagoner, president of the group Advocates for Youth. "We can't afford the luxury of denial. Abstinence-only programs are the embodiment of denial. They have been proven not to work, and it's time to invest in real sex education, including condoms."

Others praised the research for providing much-needed data in the often highly polarized debate over teenage sexuality.

The Research Disproves the Oral Sex Myth

"We have these images of oral sex parties, but it's not based on evidence. It's not based on research," said Claire Brindis, a professor of pediatrics and health policy at the University of California at San Francisco. "A study like this allows us to begin to dissect what actually is going on. It really helps to break both the positive and negative stereotypes."

Previous research had suggested that oral sex was increasing among teenagers as an alternative to intercourse, but those studies were based on small samples or anecdotal reports. The new study analyzed data collected from a nationally representative sample of 1,150 females and 1,121 males aged 15 to 19 who were questioned in detail in 2002 for the federal government's National Survey of Family Growth.

A majority of the teens—55 percent—said they had engaged in oral sex, which was slightly more than the 50 percent who said they had had vaginal sex. But oral sex was much more common among those who already had had intercourse: Eighty-seven percent of those who reported on a computerized questionaire that they had had vaginal sex said they had engaged in oral sex as well, compared with 23 percent of those who described themselves as virgins.

When the researchers examined the timing of sexual behaviors, they found that among those who said during face-to-face interviews that had had vaginal sex in the past six months, 82 percent said they also had had oral sex, compared with 26 percent of the virgins.

Among those who had initiated vaginal sex more than three years earlier, 92 percent had engaged in oral sex.

Parents should talk with their children more about a variety of sexual activities.

Jones noted that the analysis could not determine which sexual activity tended to occur first.

When the researchers examined the number of partners the teens reported, they found that among those who reported engaging in oral sex, 67 percent had only one partner, "another piece of evidence that there's not a lot of teens engaging in serial oral sex," Jones said.

Parents Are the Ultimate Influence

In addition to the implications for sex-ed classes, the findings indicate that parents should talk with their children more about a variety of sexual activities, experts said.

"When parents talk with children and teenagers about sex, they may need to broaden the number of topics they discuss," said Sarah Brown of the National Campaign to Prevent Teen and Unplanned Pregnancy, a private nonprofit advocacy group. "They have to embrace the 'ick' factor. They have to face the facts."

10

Reality Television Gives a Realistic Image of Teen Pregnancy

Amy Benfer

Amy Benfer is a writer living in San Francisco. She contributes regularly to Salon, San Francisco *magazine, and* The New York Times Book Review.

The season finale of MTV's reality show 16 and Pregnant *was a very emotional episode. Instead of glamorizing teen pregnancy, the series actually depicts the life of six pregnant teenagers fairly accurately, especially by allowing each girl to narrate her own hour-long episode. The show follows the girls as they answer tough questions for themselves. Ending with an episode focused on adoption, the show sheds a true light on the many possible outcomes of teen pregnancy.*

Last week's [July 16, 2009] season finale of the MTV reality show *16 and Pregnant* had my daughter and me sobbing together in under 10 minutes. The episode follows Catelynn and Tyler, two teenagers who decide, against the wishes of their parents, to release their daughter for adoption. The next day, a 30-second recap of the episode started us off again.

"Oh my God," said my daughter, Sydney, nearly 20. "When Catelynn says, 'I'm going to the hospital and leaving with nothing. . . .'"

Amy Benfer, "I Actually Was Sixteen and Pregnant," salon.com, July 23, 2009. This article first appeared in Salon.com, at http://www.salon.com. An online version remains in the Salon archives. Reprinted with permission.

"I know!" I said. "And when they are standing in the parking lot and the baby is gone and Tyler looks down and he's still holding the blanket!"

And there we were, reaching for the Kleenex again.

High-profile celebrity teen births, coupled with a slight ... uptick in teen birth rates have led to an all-out cultural obsession with teen and/or unwed mothers.

Teen Parenting in Pop Culture

We weren't sure what to expect when we first heard that MTV—the network that arguably started the reality TV craze with *The Real World* nearly a generation ago, the channel known for launching the second careers of Bret Michaels and Flava Flav—was planning a documentary-style series on pregnant and parenting teenagers. But we knew one thing: We were going to watch every single episode.

My daughter and I consider ourselves experts on the teen parent in pop culture for the simple [reason] that, in 1989, I became one. Back in the 1990s and into the early part of this century, when teen pregnancy rates were steadily declining (between 1991 and 2005, the rate dropped by a third), studios were perhaps a bit more open to portraying teen mothers as something other than an unmitigated tragedy: There was *90210*, in which the pregnant character, Andrea, ends up at Yale; the utterly charming, character-driven *Gilmore Girls*, in which the daughter, strangely enough, also ends up at Yale; and the weirdly revisionist version of *Riding in Cars With Boys*, in which the character played by Drew Barrymore does not end up going to college at all, unlike Beverly Donofrio, the former *Village Voice* writer whose memoir is the source for the film.

But lately, my daughter and I have had a hard time finding enough space on the TiVo to keep up: A couple of high-profile celebrity teen births, coupled with a slight (but still depressing) uptick in teen birth rates have led to an all-out cultural obsession with teen and/or unwed mothers. In this post-*Juno*/Bristol [Palin]/Jamie-Lynn [Spears] summer, we've had one patronizing ABC News *Primetime* special, hosted by Jay Schadler; a pregnant band geek on *The Secret Life of the American Teenager*; Lindsay Lohan as a fake unwed mother in the straight-to-TV movie *Labor Pains*; and, my personal favorite, *THS Investigates: Teen Pregnancy Nightmares!* a one-hour special that came in the lineup right after *When Husbands Kill!* We also had *16 and Pregnant*, a show that proved so popular that it is getting a reunion show tonight and also coming back for a second season.

The Critics Were Concerned

From the beginning, critics seemed concerned that MTV would somehow "glamorize" teen pregnancy. But I was worried more about the girls themselves: Often in our zeal to reduce teen pregnancy—a goal, I hope it goes without saying, I adamantly support—we end up unfairly reducing the girls who do become pregnant to little more than a public service announcement, as if by depicting their lives as unrelentingly bleak and unsalvageable, we will somehow scare every other teen into never having a broken condom, or even having sex in the first place. But pregnancy is just the beginning of a teen parent's story: These are actual people, with actual children, and 18 years (at least) ahead of them to continue making decisions and taking action to build their family's lives. Would MTV have the nerve to portray them in a realistic, respectful manner? Or would they end up being exploited into caricature?

As it turns out, they did a pretty good job. Six girls—two high school cheerleaders (Maci and Farrah), an Army brat (Ebony), a high school dropout whose mother is pregnant at the same time (Whitney), a party girl (Amber) and a couple considering adoption (Catelynn and Tyler)—each have a one-hour, self-contained episode that follows them for five to seven months, through pregnancy and young parenthood. They mixed it up pretty well, in terms of geography and class, but could have done a better job with racial diversity (five of the girls are white; Ebony appears to be biracial and lives with her white mother)—something we hope they fix in Season 2.

An Actual Real Look at Teen Pregnancy

One of the best aspects of the show is that each episode is narrated by the teens themselves. "The goal was for them to tell their own stories, to narrate their lives and their feelings in a way that felt organic," says executive producer Morgan J. Freeman. The girls were given small flip cameras they could use as "video diaries" to talk about their feelings in private whenever they liked. Some of the most revealing scenes between family members—an argument between Maci and her boyfriend, Ryan, en route to the doctor's office, and one that ends with Farrah's mother slapping her while driving, then telling her she's "had enough of her belligerent anti-Christ attitude"—were captured on small cameras mounted inside the subject's cars, with no crew present. "There's not really a lot of sit-down interviews," says Freeman. "It's less about asking people to talk about their feelings and more about watching the action, what actually happens."

In our zeal to reduce teen pregnancy . . . we end up unfairly reducing the girls who do because pregnant to little more than a public service announcement.

Each episode spectacularly culminates at around the 40-minute mark with a birthing scene, some of the most explicit I've seen on television. Initially, I was totally freaked out by the idea of a producer asking minor girls, even minor girls about to become parents, to consent to be filmed in stirrups, naked to the waist, in labor—but even I had to admit that it made for riveting, emotionally charged television—and certainly a heads-up to any skeptics that carrying and giving birth to a baby is a really big deal. (According to Freeman, refusing to allow cameras in the birthing room was not a "deal-breaker" and Maci, for one, chose to have her birth depicted in demure line drawings rather than real-life Technicolor.)

No one's asking teenagers to take the girls of 16 *and* Pregnant *as role models.*

The Show Raises Some Serious Questions

But the real heart of the show is the big questions: Do I stay in school, and if so, what will my friends think? Can I get my GED [General Education Development certification]? Can I go to college? Can I hold a job? Do I live with my parents, or my baby's father?

Young fathers struggle with their role, and some show real maturity and kindness. But even the bad relationships lead to some good questions (ones that, I might add, many adult women have yet to figure out): How do you get someone to step up so that the family works in everyone's best interest? When your partner is not respecting you and your child, when do you stay and hope for the best? And when do you realize you are fighting a losing battle and take steps to make it on your own? In one of the most heartbreaking moments of the series, a tearful Maci asks her boyfriend, Ryan, if they would be having all these problems if she hadn't become pregnant; Ryan, who proposed to her *before* he knew she was pregnant, tells her, "If we didn't have the baby, we wouldn't be together." By the end of her episode, Maci was still mulling over her options; we may see what she decided on tonight's reunion special.

Some Critics Are Not Being Fair

In her *New York Times* review, Ginia Bellafante dismissed these girls as "real-life Junos who are not scoring in the 99th percentile on the verbal portion of their SATs" and accused MTV of promoting "working-class voyeurism"—citing, among other things, that Amber was "at least 30 pounds overweight before she even started to show" and eats Taco Bell while in labor. She concludes that the series' "class prejudice" would believe that "if you're not setting out for [elite colleges] Wesleyan or Berkeley, then raising a child when you ought to be working on the yearbook is as good a road to character development as any."

Actually, failing to acknowledge that two of the teens—Farrah and Maci—actually are enrolled in college while mothering infants sounds like "class prejudice" to me. (Also, I hear even Ivy League college students are overweight and occasionally eat Taco Bell, too). And since she brought it up, I'd just like to point out that being a teen parent doesn't necessarily exclude one from Bellafante's exclusive club of teenagers who count: I actually went to Wesleyan with my daughter, as did *Riding in Cars With Boys* author Beverly Donofrio 20 years before me; Ariel Gore, who had her daughter at 19 and went on to write six books and found the magazine *Hip Mama*, went to Berkeley.

No one's asking teenagers to take the girls of *16 and Pregnant* as role models. But isn't it fair to give them some space to talk about their own lives, rather than be talked *about* by others who see them as statistical symbols of social decay? Wouldn't it be nice if some teens—and parents—who watch the episode in which Whitney's friends ostracize her because they are afraid "they might get pregnant, too," realize that stigmatizing this one girl's pregnancy contributed directly to her dropping out of school? I'm guessing that few teens who watch a young girl try to hold down a job, school, a place on the dance team and still have time at home with her son are going to want to swap places with her—but some of them might come out with respect, even admiration.

The Adoption Episode
Upended Expectations

The series actually managed to surprise me, too. From the beginning, I was bracing for the adoption episode, and wondering how they would handle it. Although only about 1 percent of all women choose to put their children up for adoption, it remains, in the popular imagination, one of the most palatable choices to adults who have never had to make that decision themselves: One avoids the dicey moral territory of abortion, and the equally unpopular position of being the kind of parent whom others are perfectly comfortable discriminating against. And yet the same people who urge a young girl to think of a 6-week-old fetus as a "child" can often be remarkably callous when it comes to acknowledging that giving up an actual child that one has carried for nine months and given birth to is, for most women, a much more excruciating sense of loss. In the past (when about 80 percent of young, unmarried women released their children), it was often not even much of a choice: Families and social workers presented it as the only moral option. So how would this episode play out? Would the parents really feel it was their choice? Would they acknowledge just how hard it was?

The show upended all my expectations. Catelynn and Tyler fight their own parents—who, in a twist straight out of *Gossip Girl*, married each other after their kids started dating—every step of the way. Tyler's ex-con father, Butch, tells him he is disappointed in him: "You didn't man up. You weren't the cowboy I thought you were." Catelynn's mother, April (not long ago arrested for a DUI), puts a bassinet in the front room and calls her daughter a bitch for going to see the adoption counselor without her. But both of their kids insist that the life they have isn't good enough for their child.

"The degree of their strength was not apparent to me when I first met them," says Freeman. "At first, I wasn't even sure they were going to go through with it. But you just watch Tyler carve out this safe space for him and Catelynn and their daughter and push back on the family. When I watched it, I was in awe. I thought, 'Where is this strength coming from?'"

I never expected to have a child until my 30s, and now, at 36, I am the mother of a young woman.

It's an open adoption, so the adoptive parents, Teresa and Brandon, agree to share letters and photographs and remain in contact with Tyler and Catelynn (as well as appearing on national television, of course). They also witness their grief firsthand. In the delivery room Teresa gives Catelynn a silver bracelet and promises that she, and their daughter, will wear one that matches hers, so that the three will always be linked. Then Catelynn and Tyler end up in the parking lot, watching their daughter driven away and holding her receiving blanket.

Back on the couch, Sydney and I, both wiping tears from our eyes, started laughing at how ridiculous it was that we were both sobbing over a 30-second clip. "They should have kept her," she said.

"No," I said. "This is one case where I'm sure they really knew they were doing the right thing."

The Author's Own Outcome

Sydney is now a college sophomore. She is fluent in Spanish and loves her dog. She is kind and wise. Even as a teenager, I never expected to have a child until my 30s, and now, at 36, I am the mother of a young woman. When I first became pregnant, I was certain there was no way I could do right by both of us. Nine months later I thought, yes, I think I can. And we did.

That was a long time ago. Twenty years ago, actually. Tomorrow.

11

Television Does Not Provide a Realistic Picture of Teen Pregnancy

Adele Horin

Adele Horin is a columnist and reporter for The Sydney Morning Herald.

Due to the recent onslaught of movies from Hollywood that are romanticizing unexpected and teen pregnancies, it is worrisome that some teens may be disillusioned into emulating what they are seeing. These movies are nowhere close to representing teen pregnancy in its true light, which is much harder than it is made to look. The movies misrepresent everything from adoption to single motherhood, and magazines are portraying "baby bumps" as fashion accessories, sending teens even more mixed messages. It is ultimately up to parents and educators alike to set the record straight for teens by reiterating how complicated and tough these situations actually are in real life.

Teenage girls have resisted the lure of the [Australian government's incentive to new parents] baby bonus, despite claims that the payment—worth $4,258—was fuelling a mini baby-boom among the young. Official figures show births to teenagers declined in 2006 after the bonus was introduced. (It's older women who are reproducing like rabbits).

But will teenage girls be able to resist the pro-natalist messages from a crop of recent pregnancy movies? The movies

Adele Horin, "Teen Pregnancy Made Easy with a Bit of Hollywood Gloss," *The Sydney Morning Herald*, March 29, 2008. Copyright © 2008, The Sydney Morning Herald. Reproduced by permission of the author.

cast the subject of unplanned pregnancy in such a romantic light, I am fully expecting maternity wards in November/December [2008] to be overrun by teens in labour.

Movies That Romanticise Accidental Pregnancy

In the four movies I have in mind—*Juno, Knocked Up, Waitress* and *Bella*—the single girls and young women all decide to have their babies. They all find support and live happily ever after. The Right to Life [faction] must be ecstatic. Its scary foetus videos will be redundant now that Hollywood is propounding the anti-abortion message.

I must be the last person to have caught *Juno*, the funkiest and most appealing of the pregnancy movies, whose lead, Ellen Page, was an Oscar nominee. She plays a sassy 16-year-old who gets pregnant after what she calls "premeditated sex". As they do in America, she picks from the classified ads a yuppie couple who wants to adopt a baby. It would be incorrect to say abortion is not considered.

---

*You realise it [*Juno*] is just a superior romantic comedy that bears no relationship to reality.*

Misrepresenting Abortion in *Juno*

It is, for about one minute. For someone so smart, Juno is easily put off by a visit to an abortion clinic that looks like a tattoo parlour, and by an encounter with a friend demonstrating outside.

It is all so hip and progressive—the demonstrator is no bible-bashing [Australian politician] Fred Nile lookalike but a cute, rather dipsy Korean girl, and the abortion clinic receptionist is no officious medico but comes studded with piercings, and [has] a crudely sexual turn of phrase. That's why the movie is so seductive. It goes against the grain. The witty dialogue, from stripper-turned-screenwriter Diablo Cody, is so superior to the usual American pap, you believe for a while this movie is true grit.

It is only later you realise it is just a superior romantic comedy that bears no relationship to reality. I guess some pregnant 16-year-olds are lucky to have two supportive parents, a sensitive boyfriend, and a school that allows them to attend right to the end. Perhaps there is even a girl, who on top of all these blessings, is able to give her baby up convinced it is noble to help a childless woman, and better for the child that way.

But these girls, if they exist, are few and far between. In Australia, adoptions of locally-born babies have fallen to just 59 in 2006–07 because young pregnant girls, if they do not have abortions, tend to keep their babies (the most reliable statistics—from South Australia—show 53 per cent of pregnant teens choose to terminate the pregnancy). Anyone who has read the sorrowful accounts of those forced to give their babies away before the advent of the single-parent payment in the 1970s knows the decision shattered women's lives and caused endless grief.

I know filmmakers have a right to tell any story; their job is not to deal with the representative or the typical. They are artists, not propagandists, and *Juno* is not a documentary or an educational film.

Misrepresenting Single Motherhood

But is it just coincidence that the artists behind these movies are propounding the same message, or is it timidity? The word abortion is not uttered in *Knocked Up*, although one of the dissolute characters refers to it jocularly as "shmishmortion". Pregnant Alison quickly makes up her mind to have the baby although she is smart, young, single, has just started an on-screen television career, and the father is a hopeless slob with whom she had a drunken one-night stand. Naturally, the hopeless slob grows up over the seven months, gets a job, a house, and dumps his childish mates. If only life imitated art.

Unfortunately for teenage girls in Australia, 60 per cent do not have a partner when their baby is born, according to a Queensland Health Department report.

The Australian Christian Channel was so enamoured of *Bella* it described [the film] as a "pro-life, pro-adoption" [award-winner]. Nina, unmarried and unemployed, is talked out of having an abortion by Jose. He finds her a job and introduces her to his warm-hearted Latino family. In *Waitress*, abortion is the one choice not on the menu, even though Jenna is accidentally pregnant to an abusive husband she plans to leave. A handsome gynaecologist makes everything OK.

Life, they [teens] need to know, is no Hollywood movie.

Sending Teens the Wrong Message

On top of this Hollywood fare are the teen magazines and websites that turn "baby bumps" into a fashion item, and [that] lovingly chronicle celebrity pregnancies from Cate Blanchett's to 16-year-old Jamie Lynn Spears's, Britney's sister.

Against this cultural tide of cheer, parents and educators are left to take a stand. It is up to us to remind our daughters and sons of how hard it is either to give a child away, or to raise a child before you have the maturity and the means. It can be done but life, they need to know, is no Hollywood movie. And will there ever be a Hollywood artist brave enough to do a romantic comedy about a girl who opts to terminate a pregnancy, complete with sensitive boyfriend, supportive parents, and happy-ever-after?

Organizations to Contact

The editors have compiled the following list of organizations concerned with the issues debated in this book. The descriptions are derived from materials provided by the organizations. All have publications or information available for interested readers. The list was compiled on the date of publication of the present volume; names, addresses, phone and fax numbers, and e-mail and Internet addresses may change. Be aware that many organizations take several weeks or longer to respond to inquiries, so allow as much time as possible.

Advocates for Youth

2000 M Street NW, Suite 750, Washington, DC   20036

Phone: (202) 419-3420 • Fax: (202) 419-1448

Web site: www.advocatesforyouth.org

Founded in 1980 as the Center for Population Options, Advocates for Youth has worked to promote better and more effective sexual health and education programs and policies, not only in the United States but in other countries as well. Its mission is based on rights, respect, and responsibility.

4Parents.gov

U.S. Department of Health and Human Services

Washington, DC   20201

Phone: (240) 453-2828

Web site: www.4parents.gov

4Parents.gov is a national public education campaign that makes available to parents the information to help their teenage child make informed decisions about sex. It puts an emphasis on the importance of a caring parent in the teen's life and encourages abstinence.

Avert

4 Brighton Road, West Sussex   RH13 5BA
  UK
Phone: +44 (0)1403 210202
e-mail: info@avert.org
Web site: www.avert.org

Avert is an international charity based in the United Kingdom that is working to avert the spread of AIDS and HIV through treatment, care, and education. Its Community Programme works with local organizations to improve these three factors, especially in areas where AIDS and HIV are most prevalent. Its booklet "2009: The Work of Avert" is available for download directly from its Web site as well as other information and tools to help in its mission against AIDS and HIV.

The Coalition for Positive Sexuality (CPS)

PO Box 77212, Washington, DC   20013
Phone: (773) 604-1654
Web site: www.positive.org

In 1996 CPS began as a poster project geared toward girls that encouraged them to acknowledge their sexuality, not deny it. Today it offers information about safe sex and sexually transmitted diseases. Its current publication *Just Say Yes* can be obtained by visiting its Web site.

IWannaKnow.org For Teens

American Social Health Association
Research Triangle Park, NC   27709
Phone: (919) 361-8488
e-mail: info@ashastd.org
Web site: www.iwannaknow.org

IWannaKnow.org For Teens was created by the American Social Health Association, an authority on sexually transmitted diseases (STDs). Its goal is to provide as much information as possible to teens in regard to STDs. There are also different sections on its Web site for teachers and parents to obtain information and pamphlets.

The National Campaign to Prevent Teen and Unplanned Pregnancy

1776 Massachusetts Ave. NW, Suite 200
Washington, DC   20036
Phone: (202) 478-8500 • Fax: (202) 478-8588
Web site: www.thenationalcampaign.org

The National Campaign to Prevent Teen and Unplanned Pregnancy was formed in 1996 to decrease teen pregnancy in America. By working with policy makers, the media, and state and local leaders, it provides the materials needed to educate parents, teens, and young adults on the prevention of teen pregnancy. It also works directly with teens on its Youth Online Network.

Planned Parenthood Federation of America

434 West 33rd Street, New York, NY   10001
Phone: (212) 541-7800 • Fax: (212) 245-1845
Web site: www.plannedparenthood.org

Planned Parenthood is a national organization that supports people's right to make reproductive decisions without governmental interference. It has more than 840 health centers nationwide and has also begun to expand globally by placing centers in Africa, Asia, and Latin America. From its Web site teens can search for centers in their area and browse information on many different health topics.

Sex, etc.

Answer, Piscataway, NJ   08854
e-mail: sexetc@rci.rutgers.edu
Web site: www.sexetc.org

Created by the national organization Answer, *Sex, etc.* is part of the Teen-to-Teen Sexuality Education program. Its goal is to improve the sexual health of teenagers by offering information and answers to their questions about contraception, relationships, teen pregnancy, sexually transmitted diseases (STDs) and other topics concerning sex. Its Web site offers many different tools, including a forum for discussions with other teens and videos about sexual health.

Sexuality Information and Education Council of the United States (SIECUS)

90 John Street, Suite 704, New York, NY   10038
Phone: (212) 819-9770 • Fax: (212) 819-9776
Web site: www.siecus.org

SIECUS was founded in 1964 with the goal of providing education and information regarding sexuality and sexual and reproductive health. It argues that sexuality is a part of being human and works to protect the sexual rights of everyone. Its Web site provides information about different sex education programs, as well as links to several of its publications, which are available for download at no cost.

Teen-Aid, Inc.

723 E. Jackson, Spokane, WA   99207
Phone: (509) 482-2868
Web site: www.teen-aid.org

Teen-Aid began in 1981 with the goal of reducing premarital sexual activity by stressing that the most effective way to avoid the consequences of premarital sex is through abstinence. It believes abstinence education strengthens not only the character of teens but also the relationship between teens and their parents. Its Web site offers information on abstinence education programs.

Youth Incentives

PO Box 9022
    The Netherlands
Phone: (+)31 (0)30 2332322 • Fax: (+)31 (0)30 2319387
e-mail: info@youthincentives.org
Web site: www.youthincentives.org

Youth Incentives was developed by Rutgers Nisso Group, an expert center on sexuality located in the Netherlands, and it is considered to be the international program on youth and sexuality. Its approach to reducing teen pregnancy and sexually transmitted diseases is through education and openness about the sexuality of youth. Its publications, including *Educational Programmes for Sex Offenders* and *Juvenile Sex Offenders Need Guidance* can be downloaded for free from its Web site.

Bibliography

Books

Michael J. Basso   *The Underground Guide to Teenage Sexuality: An Essential Handbook For Today's Teens and Parents.* Lanham, MD: National Book Network, 2007.

Heather Corinna   *S.E.X.: The All-You-Need-to-Know Progressive Sexuality Guide to Get You Through High School and College.* Cambridge, MA: Da Capo Press, 2007.

Ron Deboer   *Questions from the Pickle Jar: Teens and Sex.* Grand Rapids, MI: Faith Alive Christian Resources, 2008.

Michael DiMarco and Hayley DiMarco   *Almost Sex: 9 Signs You Are About to Go Too Far (or already have).* Grand Rapids, MI: Revell, 2009.

Richard M. Dudum   *What Your Mother Never Told You: A Survival Guide for Teenage Girls.* Charleston, SC: BookSurge Publishing, 2007.

L. Kris Gowen   *Sexual Decisions: The Ultimate Teen Guide (It Happened to Me).* Lanham, MD: Scarecrow Press, 2007.

Gina Guddat   *Unwrapped: Real Questions Asked by Real Girls (About Sex).* Franklin, TN: Providence Publishing Corporation, 2007.

Nikol Hasler	*Sex: A Book For Teens: An Uncensored Guide to Your Body, Sex, and Safety.* San Francisco, CA: Zest Books, 2010.
Melisa Holmes and Trish Hutchison	*Girlology Hang-Ups, Hook-Ups, and Holding Out: Stuff You Need to Know About Your Body, Sex, and Dating.* Deerfield Beach, FL: HC, 2007.
Jeanne Warren Lindsay	*Teen Dads: Rights, Responsibilities, and Joys.* Buena Park, CA: Morning Glory Press, 2008.
Justin Lookadoo	*The Dirt on Sex.* Grand Rapids, MI: Revell, 2008.
Ron Luce	*Friends Without Benefits: What Teens Need to Know About Sex.* Ventura, CA: Regal Books, 2010.
Rolf McEwen	*Teen Sexuality: A Humorous Guide to a Serious Matter.* Shelbyville, KY: Wasteland Press, 2009.
Ruth Westheimer and Pierre Lehu	*Dr. Ruth's Guide to Teens and Sex Today: From Social Networking to Friends with Benefits.* New York, NY: Teachers College Press, 2008.

Periodicals

Jacob M. Appel	"Embracing Teenage Sexuality: Let's Rethink the Age of Consent," *Huffington Post*, January 1, 2010.
Lauren Bell	"Let's Talk About Teen Sex," *Reader's Digest*, March 2008.

Janice Shaw Crouse — "Reducing Teen Pregnancies and Abortions," Townhall.com, September 8, 2008.

Steve Doughty — "Most Teenage Pregnancies Now End with an Abortion," *MailOnline*, May 11, 2009.

Ellen Goodman — "The Truth About Teens and Sex," *Boston Globe*, January 3, 2009.

Peter Hitchens — "More Sex Education Means More Teenage Pregnancies . . . Always," *MailOnline*, March 3, 2010.

Aaron Igdalsky — "Middle School Birth Control Is Absurd," *Daily Campus*, October 23, 2007.

Meg James and Dawn C. Chmielewski — "Teen Sex in 'Secret Life' Births Debate Over ABC Family Values," *Los Angeles Times*, February 1, 2009.

Sarah Kliff — "Teen Pregnancy, Hollywood Style," *Newsweek*, July 23, 2008.

Tamar Lewin — "Rethinking Sex Offender Laws for Youth Texting," *New York Times*, March 20, 2010.

Belinda Luscombe — "The Truth About Teen Girls," *Time*, September 11, 2008.

William McGurn — "Like a Virgin: The Press Take on Teenage Sex," *Wall Street Journal*, January 6, 2009.

Alice Park   "Parents' Sex Talk with Kids: Too Little, Too Late," *Time*, December 7, 2009.

Tara Parker-Pope   "The Myth of Rampant Teenage Promiscuity," *New York Times*, January 26, 2009.

William Saletan   "Good Judgement: Let's Be Frank About Teen Sex and Abortion," *Slate*, January 22, 2008.

Rob Stein   "Teen Sex Rates Stop Falling, Data Show," *Washington Post*, July 22, 2007.

Joanna Sugden   "Pupils to Be Forced to Have Sex Education Under Age of Consent," *TimesOnline*, November 5, 2009.

Peter Tatchell   "Lowering the Unrealistic Age of Consent Will Help Teens," *Independent.ie*, March 10, 2008.

Jessica Valenti   "Abstinence Double Standard Threaten's Girl's Health," *AlterNet*, December 29, 2009.

Samantha Wender   "New Teen Parents Forced to Grow Up Fast," *ABC News*, June 17, 2009.

Index